WOMAN'S HOUR 50th ANNIVERSARY POETRY COLLECTION

Pat McLoughlin was born in ... ..., Hampshire, in 1933, of a French mother and Irish father. After leaving school at eighteen she worked as a bank clerk and then joined the Women's Royal Naval Service. She was commissioned as a third officer, but left when she married in 1957. Two years later she joined the BBC as a studio manager and in 1970 she became Producer of the *Woman's Hour* serial story. She edited and produced over 500 serials until her retirement in 1993, the year she was awarded an MBE and was a Whitbread Prize judge.

Pat McLoughlin edited the first *Woman's Hour Book of Short Stories* in 1990, followed by a second volume in 1992. Both are available as BBC Radio Collection cassettes, as are over a dozen original *Woman's Hour* serials which she has produced, including the *Woman's Hour Jane Austen Collection*. She continues to produce serials and cassette readings as a freelance producer, and in 1993 she put together a compilation of John Betjeman's poetry, read by the poet, for the BBC.

WOMAN'S HOUR
50th Anniversary Poetry Collection

EDITED BY PAT McLOUGHLIN

PENGUIN BOOKS
BBC BOOKS

PENGUIN BOOKS
BBC BOOKS

Published by the Penguin Group and BBC Worldwide Ltd
Penguin Books Ltd, 27 Wrights Lane, London W8 5TZ, England
Penguin Books USA Inc., 375 Hudson Street, New York, New York 10014, USA
Penguin Books Australia Ltd, Ringwood, Victoria, Australia
Penguin Books Canada Ltd, 10 Alcorn Avenue, Toronto, Ontario, Canada M4V 3B2
Penguin Books (NZ) Ltd, 182–190 Wairau Road, Auckland 10, New Zealand

Penguin Books Ltd, Registered Offices: Harmondsworth, Middlesex, England

First published 1996
1 3 5 7 9 10 8 6 4 2

The acknowledgements on p. 209 constitute an extension
of this copyright page

🅱🅱🅲™ BBC used under licence

Printed in England by Clays Ltd, St Ives plc

CONTENTS

POST-WAR

MOTHERS

MATING CALLS

POEMS ABOUT SEX

ALL OF THE LONELY ONES

AGAINST COUPLING

THE OTHER SIDE OF THE STORY

SO MANY KINDS OF AWFUL MEN

THEMES FOR WOMEN

IN SUMMER

THE WORLD AWRY

THE BEGINNING OF AUTUMN

WHEN YOU MOVE OUT

FRIENDSHIP

THE OLD FOLK

IN THE BLEAK MID-WINTER

INTRODUCTION

I was asked to select the poems for this anthology of women poets for two reasons. Firstly, I produced the *Woman's Hour* serial for many years, during which period, in 1990 and 1992, I edited two volumes of *Woman's Hour Short Stories*. In addition, I also produced some poetical sound pictures on a number of themes. These sound pictures reintroduced me to the joys of poetry, a pleasure I have rediscovered over the past few months, working on this selection. During this time, I have studied with a certain partisan interest what other editors of poetry anthologies have had to say about their selection and their motivation for that selection. Of them, two particular statements spoke to me – neither, as it happens, from introductions to collections exclusively of women's poetry. The first is from the introduction to *Poems on the Underground* (Cassell, 1992). The editors wrote: 'The great subjects are well represented here: love, death, war, the natural world, time, memory. But these are not the only themes of poetry . . . there is also a fine tradition of comic verse, and in amongst the passion and nostalgia we placed a few banana skins.' I should like to feel that the same can be said about the collection you will find here.

The second statement which reverberated with me comes from what must seem like a fairly unlikely source – a 'preliminary note' by General Sir John Hackett to *Poems of the Second World War* (Dent, 1985) from which, incidentally, comes Elsie Cawser's 'Salvage Song (or: The Housewife's Dream)' – a charming 'banana skin' if ever there was one! The General identified war poetry as poetry 'such as would be unlikely to be written *except* in wartime' and, increasingly, I felt that much of the content of this anthology, particularly the poems written by women over the last fifty years or so, would not have been written but for their womanhood.

Of course this is patently obvious where the subject is menstruation, childbirth or the menopause, events which can *only* be experienced by women. But it applies, too, to all-embracing themes such as marriage, love, death, war, friendship, even masturbation (oh the wicked humour of Fleur Adcock's 'Against Coupling') – to many things that men also experience, yet write about differently or not at all. I have highlighted the last fifty-odd years because, in trawling through earlier women's poetry, it struck me how much the writers almost strove to be token men – victims as ever, maybe, albeit unconsciously, of male attitudes which underrate female values and at the same time pursue their own goals in a 'masterly' selfish fashion. Two poems in this collection – Lynn Peters' 'Why Dorothy Wordsworth is not as Famous as her Brother' and U. A. Fanthorpe's 'The Poet's Companion' – illustrate this latter problem much more vividly than I can.

And indeed, it is time to move on to the poems themselves. But first a word or two about the order in which you will find them. Having selected between 150 and 200 poems, I found it essential to decide on some sort of thematic plan. I didn't want to present the poems alphabetically – a comprehensive index can take care of any resulting frustration in immediately locating a poem – nor did I want to present them chronologically. No, the more I looked at the poems, the more it seemed that what was largely emerging was the *seasons* in a woman's life, as well as some wonderful poems about the seasons of the year themselves and therefore the order of the poems should be a procession through the calendar year with these two objectives in mind. Elizabeth Bartlett's wonderful poem 'Themes for Women' encapsulates my aim in this collection far better than I can. Of course there are some poems too good to miss that don't fit comfortably into this format, and these I have interpolated as 'comments'.

It is invidious to pick out and mention some poems from such a large and distinguished gathering. But I felt I might select some that have particularly 'spoken' to me or caught my interest in some way. Firstly, it was a pleasant discovery to find that 'The Gate of the Year', so popularized by George VI's 1939 Christmas broadcast ('And I said to the man who stood at the gate of the year:"Give me a light, that I may tread safely into the unknown!"') was actually written by a woman, M. Louise Haskins (1875–1957); as indeed was 'Solitude', which produced the splendid cliché, 'Laugh, and the world laughs with you,/ Weep and you weep alone,' written by Ella Wheeler Wilcox (1850–1919), which, like most clichés, is true.

The spring poems contain an old favourite of mine – 'I so liked Spring' by Charlotte Mew (1869–1928) – surely one of the best evocations of disappointed love ever, so simple and moving in its rhythmic brevity.

In view of the recent overkill of war anniversaries, serious thought has been given to how much poetry about war to include. At the same time *women* writing about their war experiences have not had nearly as much exposure as male poets, and much that has been written by women is universal in its theme, as applicable to Bosnia or Northern Ireland now as it was to the Second World War fifty years ago. Some, too, are delightful mood-breakers, like, for instance, 'In the Beginning was the Word' by Sheila Parry (b. 1933) in which the poet recalls that in 1939, 'When I was six I wanted war', and thus when war began, 'It wasn't Hitler started war,/I knew that it was me.' Another welcome moment of light relief is supplied by 'To a Barrage Balloon' by May Morton: 'We used to say "If pigs could fly!"/And now they do.'

But naturally it is the serious moments that make the most impact. In 'Seaman, 1941' by Molly Holden (1927–81), a small island community receives back one of its sons, washed up on its shores following a torpedo attack: 'old men who had fished with his father/and grandfather and knew him at once . . .'; in 'Pictures from the Blitz' Lois Clark (who drove a stretcher-party car during the London blitz) recalls, 'I can still close my eyes and see/her sitting there,/in her big armchair,/. . .

framed by the jagged lines of her broken house', vividly recalling to me – like Sheila Parry, a child in the last war – a newsreel of the bombing of Coventry and an old woman being lifted out of her ruined home, a rictus smile frozen on her face. And the horrors of the holocaust have rarely been expressed more movingly for me than in Evangeline Paterson's 'History Teacher in the Warsaw Ghetto Rising' 'leading his scattered handful/of scarecrow twelve-year-olds/towards the last ten minutes/of their own brief history'.

Reconsidering the war section of this collection reminds me of another satisfaction: bringing together two opposite aspects of the same issue. 'Post-War' by Libby Houston (b. 1941) and 'I've Worked it Out' by Susanne Ehrhardt (b. 1944) both feature fathers lost in the war, though serving on opposite sides. Both were 'unaccounted for': 'still I don't know/where my father/flying home/took a wrong turning' (Libby Houston). For Susanne Ehrhardt's mother there was the added agony of prolonged hope that her husband might be a prisoner of war in Russia. 'In '55, Adenauer negotiated the release/of the last POW's in Soviet hands./Aged eleven, I watched her watch the trains go by./ Leaning from open wagons other men waved to us,/. . . It was then she gave up and wept.'

I was gratified to bring together a more light-hearted theme with 'The Frog Prince' by Stevie Smith (1902–71): 'do other enchanted people feel as nervous/As I do?' This endearing reptilian shyness is tartly offset by Marge Piercy's 'A Story Wet as Tears': 'Though courtship turns frogs into princes,/marriage turns them quietly back.'

I must just mention a few more 'showstoppers' as far as I am concerned. Firstly 'Annunciation' by Sylvia Kantaris (b. 1936): 'If they should canonise me/(setting me up as chaste and meek and mild)/God only knows what nonsense/they'll visit on the child'; secondly, Sheila Parry's 'August Afternoon', surely one of the most vivid portraits of babyhood and hot sunny days on the beach: 'Vague memories of salty kisses,/paddled toes/Are locked forever in their minds/As they are carried home.'

'Penguin on the Beach' by Ruth Miller (1919–69) carries a very different message – the damage we have done to our world. ('He eats/ Fish from his Saviour's hands, and it tastes black.') How moving, too, is 'Urban Lyric' by Elaine Feinstein (b. 1930), in which an ordinary woman ('The gaunt lady of the service wash') celebrates her survival from cancer: 'This morning she tastes sunshine in the dusty air./And she is made alert to the day's beauty,/as if her terror had wakened poetry.'

The notes I made about the poems I wanted to feature in this introduction are in a 1992 diary which carries the quote from Woody Allen 'It's not that I'm afraid to die. I just don't want to be there when it happens', bringing me neatly to the last part of this anthology, age and death. There are many moving examples but I feel I have to pick out 'Let the Snow Cover Her' by Janet Caird (b. 1913): 'Let the snow cover her./She is too old to follow the sledge/. . . the silence and cold/ will lull her to sleep./Let the snow cover her.' And, finally, how could I not include 'Warning' by Jenny Joseph? Firstly because it is a fine poem and a great shout of positive affirmation about old age; secondly because it was the poem most frequently mentioned to me whenever anyone learned I had embarked on this anthology. It also carries the message I want this selection to convey – that poetry is for everyone. It is immediate and succinct, moving and funny, not at all obscure or 'difficult', and wonderful in the richness of its language and imagery.

Would that novels were being written the way poetry is today!

Pat McLoughlin

POETRY

MARIANNE MOORE (1887–1972)

Poetry

I, too, dislike it.
   Reading it, however, with a perfect contempt for it, one
discovers in
    it, after all, a place for the genuine.

The Uncertainty of the Poet

I am a poet.
I am very fond of bananas.

I am bananas.
I am very fond of a poet.

I am a poet of bananas.
I am very fond.

A fond poet of 'I am, I am' –
Very bananas.

Fond of 'Am I bananas?
Am I?' – a very poet.

Bananas of a poet!
Am I fond? Am I very?

Poet bananas! I am.
I am fond of a 'very'.

I am of very fond bananas.
Am I a poet?

THE GATE OF THE YEAR

M. LOUISE HASKINS (1875–1957)

The Gate of the Year

And I said to the man who stood at the gate of the year:
'Give me a light, that I may tread safely into the unknown!'
And he replied:
'Go out into the darkness and put your hand into the Hand of God.
That shall be to you better than light and safer than a known way.'

So, I went forth, and finding the Hand of God, trod gladly into the night
And He led me toward the hills and the breaking of day in the lone East.

So, heart, be still!
What need our little life,
Our human life, to know,
If God hath comprehension?
In all the dizzy strife
Of things both high and low
God hideth His intention.

New Year Snow

For three days we waited,
a bowl of dull quartz for sky.
At night the valley dreamed of snow,
lost Christmas angels with dark-white wings
flailing the hills.
I dreamed a poem, perfect
as the first five-pointed flake,
that melted at dawn:
a Janus-time
to peer back at guttering dark days,
trajectories of the spent year.
And then snow fell.
Within an hour, a world immaculate
as January's new-hung page.
We breathe the radiant air like men new-born.
The children rush before us.
As in a dream of snow
we track through crystal fields
to the green horizon
and the sun's reflected rose.

February

Winter. Time to eat fat
and watch hockey. In the pewter mornings, the cat,
a black fur sausage with yellow
Houdini eyes, jumps up on the bed and tries
to get onto my head. It's his
way of telling whether or not I'm dead.
If I'm not, he wants to be scratched; if I am
he'll think of something. He settles
on my chest, breathing his breath
of burped-up meat and musty sofas,
purring like a washboard. Some other tomcat,
not yet a capon, has been spraying our front door,
declaring war. It's all about sex and territory,
which are what will finish us off
in the long run. Some cat owners around here
should snip a few testicles. If we wise
hominids were sensible, we'd do that too,
or eat our young, like sharks.
But it's love that does us in. Over and over
again, *He shoots, he scores!* and famine
crouches in the bedsheets, ambushing the pulsing
eiderdown, and the windchill factor hits
thirty below, and pollution pours
out of our chimneys to keep us warm.
February, month of despair,
with a skewered heart in the centre.
I think dire thoughts, and lust for French fries
with a splash of vinegar.
Cat, enough of your greedy whining
and your small pink bumhole.
Off my face! You're the life principle,
more or less, so get going
on a little optimism around here.
Get rid of death. Celebrate increase. Make it be spring.

I so liked Spring

I so liked Spring last year
    Because you were here; –
      The thrushes too –
Because it was these you so liked to hear –
      I so liked you.

This year's a different thing, –
    I'll not think of you.
But I'll like Spring because it is simply Spring
    As the thrushes do.

BLACK-OUT

CHARLOTTE MEW (1869–1928)

···

May, 1915

Let us remember Spring will come again
      To the scorched, blackened woods, where the
          wounded trees
Wait with their old wise patience for the heavenly rain,
Sure of the sky: sure of the sea to send its healing breeze,
    Sure of the sun. And even as to these
        Surely the Spring, when God shall please,
    Will come again like a divine surprise
To those who sit today with their great Dead, hands in their
   hands, eyes in their eyes,
At on with Love, at one with Grief: blind to the scattered things
   and changing skies.

In the Beginning was the Word

When I was six I wanted war.
Obsessed with words,
I asked my Mother to explain.
She tried, but failed,
'I wish there would be war', I wailed
And wondered at her anger
And why her face was pale.

The time was 1939,
There wasn't long to wait;
The world blamed Adolf Hitler
But I knew who called down fate,
My greed to taste the apple
From the forbidden tree.
It wasn't Hitler started war,
I knew that it was me.

Peace was just another word,
Lost in myth and fable;
As strange and distant to us then
As Arthur and his table.
Still it eludes our feeble grasp
As the sword sinks in the lake.

We had a holiday for Peace,
Not knowing it was fake.
A feast of parties in the street
When all the neighbours came.
But the Lord of the Dance
Had nails in His feet
And the great white bird was lame.

The War Generation: Ave

In cities and in hamlets we were born,
    And little towns behind the van of time;
A closing era mocked our guileless dawn
    With jingles of a military rhyme.
But in that song we heard no warning chime,
    Nor visualised in hours benign and sweet
The threatening woe that our adventurous feet
    Would starkly meet.

Thus we began, amid the chaos blown
    Across our childhood from an earlier war,
Too dim, too soon forgotten, to dethrone
    Those dreams of happiness we thought secure;
While imminent and fierce outside the door,
    Watching a generation grow to flower,
The fate that held our youth within its power
    Waited its hour.

Immensity

You go at night into immensity,
Leaving this green earth, where hawthorn flings
Pale stars on hedgerows, and our serenity
Is twisted into strange shapes; my heart never sings
Now on spring mornings, for you fly at nightfall
From this earth I know
Toward the clear stars, and over all
Those dark seas and waiting towns you go;
And when you come to me
There are fearful dreams in your eyes,
And remoteness. Oh, God! I see
How far away you are,
Who may so soon meet death beneath an alien star.

The Black-Out

I never feared the darkness as a child,
For then night's plumy wings that wrapped me round
Seemed gentle, and all earthly sound,
Whether man's movement or the wild,
Small stirrings of the beasts and trees, was kind,
So I was well contented to be blind.

But now the darkness is a time of dread,
Of stumbling, fearful progress, when one thinks,
With angry fear, that those dull amber chinks,
Which tell of life where all things else seem dead,
Are full of menace as a tiger's eyes
That watch our passing, hungry for the prize.

Over all Europe lies this shuddering night.
Sometimes it quivers like a beast of prey,
All tense to spring, or, trembling, turns at bay
Knowing itself too weak for force or flight,
And in all towns men strain their eyes and ears,
Like hunted beasts, for warning of their fears.

First News Reel: September 1939

It was my war, though it ended
When I was ten: could I know or guess
What the talking really said?
– 'Over the top. At the front.
Sealed-with-a-loving-kiss.
Train-loads of wounded men
At the old seaside station.
Two million dead' –
Child of the nightmare-crying 'Never again'.

The same 'I' sits here now
In this silent throng
Watching with dull surprise
Guns limbering to the line
Through umber sheaves,
Guns topped with dappled boys
And crowned with beckoning leaves,
Like floats for some harvest home
Of corn or wine;

A self removed and null
Doubting the eye that sees
The gun in its green bower,
Yet meticulously records
At each load, discharge, recoil,
How the leaves spin from the trees
In an untimely shower
Over the sunlit fields, and are whirled away
To the edge of the sky.

No mud. No wounds. No tears.
No nightmare cries. Is it possible
It could be different this time?
Far-off that passing bell
Tolls 'Different.
Yes always different. Always the same':
As the guns roar and recoil
And the leaves that spin from the trees
Deck boys for a festival.

VALENTINE ACKLAND (1906–68)

Black-Out

Night comes now
Without the artistry of hesitation, the surprising
Last minute turn-aside into a modulation,
Without the rising
Final assertion of promise before the fall.
Darkness now
Comes by routine of cardboard shutter, rattle of curtain,
Comes like a sentence everyone's learnt to utter,
Undoubted and certain,
Too stupid to interest anyone at all.

To a Barrage Balloon

We used to say 'If pigs could fly!'
       And now they do.
I saw one sailing in the sky
Some thousand feet above his sty,
       A fat one, too!
I scarcely could believe my eyes,
So just imagine my surprise
To see so corpulent a pig
Inconsequently dance a jig
       Upon a cloud.
And, when elated by the show
I clapped my hands and called 'Bravo!'
       He turned and bowed.
Then, all at once, he seemed to flop
And dived behind a chimney-top
       Out of my sight.
'He's down' thought I; but not at all,
'Twas only pride that had the fall:
       To my delight
He rose, quite gay and debonair,
Resolved to go on dancing there
       Both day and night.

       So pigs can fly,
       They really do,
This chap, though anchored in the slime,
Could reach an altitude sublime –
       A pig, 'tis true!
       I wish I knew
Just how not only pigs but men
Might rise to nobler heights again
       Right in the blue
       And start anew!

Strangers Passing:
In memory of my grandparents

They scuttle
To take their places
In the deathtrains.
Taut grey faces.

My videotapes are worn
Thin and pale. Jews
Surge on, but I can
Halt them – Still/Pause:

Check each face.
Not yet. One day they'll pass
And I will know them.
Or will not.

Young Lady Dancing with Soldier

Young lady dancing with soldier,
Feeling stern peaty cloth with your slight hand,
So very happy,
So happy
To be dancing with the patriotic male –
You have forgotten
deliberately
(Or perhaps you were never concerned to know)
Last month your partner was a shipping clerk.

How, as he sat by his few inches of window,
This boy dreamed of ships and far engagements,
Battles with purpose
and future,
Fair women without guile, and England's honour,
Comme chevalier
sans peur . . .
But instead he got conscripted into the Army,
And now you are the last symbol of his dream.

It is rather thrilling to be a last symbol,
Before mud clogs the ears, blood frets the mouth
Of the poor clerk
turned soldier,
Whose highest fortune will be to find himself
Conscripted back
to life . . .
Done up like a battered brown paper parcel –
No gentleman, *malgré tout*; clerk unemployed.

War Casualty in April

If Man has forgotten tenderness, yet it remains
With the birds feeding the anxious fluttering young.
If Man has rejected compassion, still there persists
As of old the heart-wrenching droop in missel-thrush song.
And Man dreams not of faithfulness such as the lilac tree
Flaunts undismayed beside the broken home.

The brown-coated bulb lay tombed in the drowsing earth
But never forgot its springtime tryst with Life;
Yet Man keeps no tryst with Life: he obliterates
Memory, and hope; he labours to destroy;
Serves Death; cages the iridescent wings,
Gags back the golden song, crucifies love;
Mercy denies.

    Yet the mercy of the grass
Warm sweetness breathes into this dying face,
And the tender charity of the gentle rain
Washes away the blood from these death-clouded eyes.

Cessation of War

Will it cease, and the snow,
Gathering on the muzzles of guns,
Lie undisturbed
While the lights of Europe leap and glow
On the cracking of ice as the pent-up waters flow
Bear back our sons?

Will spring see the cessation,
Pale petals flung under their feet
As they come back,
And the budding hopes of a nation
And the smiles and songs and tears which need no explanation
Fill every street?

Will midnight seem hollow,
Warm, soundless, summery, wingless skies,
And they who flew,
Knowing moonlight as a guide to show
Flat silvered roofs and factory chimneys spread below,
See with new eyes?

Will the great news be shouted
Above the sound of threshing wheat,
Bright leaves like flags,
And burdened orchards golden and red,
From toil and strife to green quiet ways to turn instead
Our eager feet?

Epitaph on a Soldier

In some far field my true-love lies,
His flooded heartblood growing cold;
The mask of death is on his eyes,
His life this day for freedom sold.

Nor will his loss remembered be,
When others desecrate the truth
In later years, except by me –
For with his passing went my youth.

The Infinite Debt

A stranger died for me,
  Groaned and dropped and died somewhere –
His fire quenched utterly
  In a shrivelling air.

And how shall I requite
  His wounds, his death, who dies unknown
And keeps my feeble flame alight
  With ransom of his own?

All life, all love's his fee
  Whose perished fire conserves my spark,
Who bought the brightening day for me
  And for himself, the dark.

Ditty

If this town should tumble down
No one would be sorry.
We'd take to the fields
And have our meals
Of bracken and prickly holly.

If these spires should once be mired
In rubble dust and water
We'd sail like ducks
Past all the clocks
And gaily shop by barter.

If we should lack a cloth to our backs
Huddled in earth together
The life of man
Is quickly spanned
And earth goes on for ever.

Seaman, 1941

This was not to be expected.

Waves, wind, and tide brought him again
to Barra. Clinging to driftwood many hours
the night before, he had not recognised
the current far off-shore his own nor
known he drifted home. He gave up, anyway,
some time before the smell of land reached out
or dawn outlined the morning gulls.

                              They found him
on the white sand southward of the ness,
not long enough in the sea to be
disfigured, cheek sideways as in sleep,
old men who had fished with his father
and grandfather and knew him at once,
before they even turned him on his back, by the set
of the dead shoulders, and were shocked.

This was not to be expected.

His mother, with hot eyes, preparing the parlour
for his corpse, would have preferred, she thought,
to have been told by telegram rather
than so to know that convoy, ship, and son
had only been a hundred miles north-west
of home when the torpedoes struck.
She could have gone on thinking that
he'd had no chance; but to die offshore,
in Hebridean tides, as if he'd stayed
a fisherman for life and never gone to war
was not to be expected.

Leave Poem

O let the days spin out
In leisure, as the clouds pass;
Weave webs of shadow
Across the grass.

Let nothing touch me now,
But the minty mountain air,
Sun, wind and your fingers
Through my hair.

And when the hills grow cold
Outside, lock out the night,
Tell me long tales and stir
The fire bright.

For I would be bastioned here
Against the constant hum
Of streets and men and ships
Whence we have come.

So let the days spin out
In magic hours and laughter
That I may hold the thought
Long, long after.

Salvage Song (or: The Housewife's Dream)

My saucepans have all been surrendered,
The teapot is gone from the hob,
The colander's leaving the cabbage
For a very much different job.
So now, when I hear on the wireless
Of Hurricanes showing their mettle,
I see, in a vision before me,
A Dornier chased by my kettle.

FRANCES CORNFORD (1886–1960)

Autumn Blitz

Unshaken world! Another day of light
After the human chaos of the night;
Although a heart in mendless horror grieves,
What calmly yellow, gently falling leaves!

It's All Very Well Now

It's all very well now, but when I'm an old lady
I think I shall be amazed, and even a bit annoyed maybe,
when I look back at these years of ceaseless effort
and consider what I did to keep my country free.

If only I were making munitions, or had joined the Forces,
my grandchildren, I know, would not think I'd fought in vain,
but why on earth I did some of the things I am doing now
will be so terribly tiresome to explain.

How can I convince them that it was to England's good
that I went to Waterloo to meet two goats travelling from Camberley,
and drove them in a car across to Victoria, where I put them in another train,
third class, non-smoker of course, to Amberley?

Why, do you suppose, when London was burning,
did I find myself alone with a Church Army lady from Rye,
and why did we do nothing at all except drink port and lemon?
(She had a dish-cover on her head, tied on with a Zingari tie.)

And will my children believe me when I tell them
that I carried a flame within me that no mortal power could dowse,
not even when I was made to take a vanload of corsets and molasses
to confuse already hopelessly confused Admirals at Trinity House?

I must confess I sometimes get a bit confused myself.
Why am I doing this? I ask and wonder – why in Britain's name did I
    do that?
Did I really imagine it would lead us grimly forward to Victory
to share my smoked-salmon sandwiches with the Home Office cat?

All my little war stories will sound so frivolous.
'The old lady is getting very frail,' they will say – 'very soft in the brain';
But I shall nod my head and say, 'Believe me, my children,
in my young days everybody was automatically quite insane'.

Love Among the Ruins of London

In the desolated alleys near Saint Paul's
Dust still falls,
And by Paternoster Row, the bookman's haunt,
Ruins gaunt
Stand uncovered, as though mourning Fleet Street's pride –
Lost Saint Bride.

But in city wastes are churches once concealed,
Now revealed –
All the squalid blocks that hid their ancient stone
Overthrown –
And the quiet benediction of a sunset fires
Wounded spires.

Pricking up between the paving, shoots of green
Now are seen;
In a sheltered niche a bird finds spartan rest
For her nest –
There is love among the ruins; after strife
There is life.

Toast

All the way back from the air field
Along the jolting road,
Past the paddy fields
And the mud-covered water-buffalo,
I have been pretending to myself
That I am not thinking about letters.
At the door of Regulating I pause,
It is a creed with me never to look for a letter,
If there is one for me it will find me.
Today, feeling bad-tempered, I defy my creed
But there is no letter.
I walk up to the mess.
Irrationally I can feel hot tears in my eyes.
I concentrate on the thought of toast for tea,
Hot toast and lots of butter,
Even jam.
It is something to look forward to for almost ten minutes.
No one answers when I speak,
They are deep in their letters.
I pour milk into my tea and wait for the toast.
They laugh over their letters, and read excerpts,
From a sister in Australia,
From a friend in hospital,
From a friend in France,
I think hard about the toast.
There is no jam but meat paste
And a soft-looking paw-paw which I don't like.
The toast is as good as I know it will be
I crunch it slowly
And the butter runs on to my fingers
And I try not to listen to Wren shop,
To the details of the friend's illness,
To the delinquencies of the dhobi.

I am a little afraid, for when the toast is finished
There will be nothing to look forward to,
And so it was yesterday
And so it will be tomorrow.

MARJORIE BATTCOCK

The Refugee

Mud dark above the stream the factory's finger
Points through the rain towards a sodden sky,
Setting and cold crush her desire to linger,
Barred shops and shuttered windows mute the street,
The scene's decay is like an ugly cry.

She turns towards her home, a furnished room,
Its paint beer-brown, its three-piece, saxe-blue plush,
Where a bald light diminishes the gloom,
But leaves her chilled, and turns her thoughts towards,
The foreign city that was once her home, lush

In the summer with grape-green linden trees;
Evenings of music, cafés, interchange
Of differing views; all this she sees,
Vivid in retrospect, each richly-textured day
Ended with war; instead the pinchbeck range

Of work's monotony, that dims her pride
In memories. But for this isolation
She blames herself – friends have been tortured, died,
She, rootless, without future, should be glad,
And being so, deny her desolation.

Bomb Incident

Stretcher to stretcher still they came,
Young and old all looked the same –
Grimed and battered
Bleeding and shattered
And who they were it hardly mattered.
Where shall we put
The dogs and cats
The budgerigar
And the cricket bat?

Remnants of lives and forever lost days,
Families ended, minds that were dazed,
Clutched to the breast
Was all they had left
Of life that had gone and homes that were wrecked.
Where shall we put
The shopping bag
The picture of Grandma
The doll of rag?

Covered with dirt and with soot and with dust –
How to begin to clean them up,
To uncover the faces,
Identify people
When nothing is left of human features.
What shall we say
To the waiting friends?
How shall we know
Such anonymous ends?

And some are so still in the hospital beds
Who is dying and who is dead?
The dead must be moved
To make room for the living
But how tell the children tearfully clinging?
What can we say
As they call to a mother?
Or, dead on a stretcher,
A sister or brother.

Whom shall we blame for the folly of war?
Whom shall we tell these stories for?
Who will believe
The sadness of death,
The terror, the fear, and the emptiness –
What can they know
Of the vacant eyes
The sorrow too deep
In the heart that dies?

MABEL ESTHER ALLAN (b. 1915)

I Saw a Broken Town

(March, 1941, after the bombing of Wallasey)

I saw a broken town beside the grey March sea,
Spray flung in the air and no larks singing,
And houses lurching, twisted, where the chestnut trees
Stand ripped and stark; the fierce wind bringing
The choking dust in clouds along deserted streets,
Shaking the gaping rooms, the jagged, raw-white stone.
Seeking for what in this quiet, stricken town? It beats
About each fallen wall, each beam, leaving no livid, aching place alone.

The 'Monstrous Regiment'

What hosts of women everywhere I see!
I'm sick to death of them – and they of me.
(The few remaining men are small and pale –
War lends a spurious value to the male.)
Mechanics are supplanted by their mothers;
Aunts take the place of artisans and others;
Wives sell the sago, daughters drive the van,
Even the mansion is without a man!
Females are farming who were frail before,
Matrons attending meetings by the score,
Maidens are minding multiple machines,
And virgins vending station-magazines.
Dames, hoydens, wenches, harridans and hussies
Cram to congestion all the trams and buses;
Misses and grandmas, mistresses and nieces,
Infest bombed buildings, picking up the pieces.
Girls from the South and lassies from the North,
Sisters and sweethearts, bustle back and forth.
The newsboy and the boy who drives the plough:
Postman and milkman – all are ladies now.
Doctors and engineers – yes, even these –
Poets and politicians, all are shes.
(The very beasts that in the meadows browse
Are ewes and mares, heifers and hens and cows. . . .)
All, doubtless, worthy to a high degree;
But oh, how boring! Yes, including me.

History Teacher in the Warsaw Ghetto Rising

The schoolmaster once known as
Umbrella Feet
unfolds his six foot length
of gangling bone

and, mild as usual,
blinks – his bi-focals
having gone the way of his pipe
and his tree-shaded study
and his wife Charlotte –

jacket flapping, as usual,
carpet slippers treading
rubble of smashed cellars,

holding his rifle uncertainly
as if he thought it irrelevant
– as indeed it is –

advances steadily into the
glare of the burning street

leading his scattered handful
of scarecrow twelve-year-olds

towards the last ten minutes
of their own brief history.

Picture from the Blitz

After all these years
I can still close my eyes and see
her sitting there,
in her big armchair,
grotesque under an open sky,
framed by the jagged lines of her broken house.

Sitting there,
a plump homely person,
steel needles still in her work-rough hands;
grey with dust, stiff with shock,
but breathing,
no blood or distorted limbs;
breathing, but stiff with shock,
knitting unravelling on her apron'd knee.

They have taken the stretchers off my car
and I am running
under the pattering flack
over a mangled garden;
treading on something soft
and fighting the rising nausea –
only a far-flung cushion, bleeding feathers.

They lift her gently
out of her great armchair,
tenderly,
under the open sky,
a shock-frozen woman trailing khaki wool.

To Billy, My Son
(Killed in Action, 15 May 1945)

Now comes, indeed, the end of all delight,
The end of forward-looking on life's way,
The end of all desire to pierce the night
For gleam of hope, the end of all things gay;
The end of any promise Spring might hold,
The end of praying and, O God, the end
Of love that waited to be shared and told;
Now, evermore, shall life with sorrow blend;
That sorrow whose dark shape the months had fought,
And strictly kept in confines of the will;
Had held quiescent while each conscious thought
Searched far horizons where joy lingered still;
But, my beloved, fearless, gallant, true,
Here is fair end of sorrow, now, for you.

POST-WAR

LIBBY HOUSTON (b. 1941)

Post-War

In 1943
my father
dropped bombs on the continent

I remember
my mother
talking about bananas
in 1944

when it rained,
creeping alone to the windowsill,
I stared up the hill,
watching, watching,
watching without a blink
for the Mighty Bananas
to stride through the blitz

they came in paper bags
in neighbours' hands
when they came
and took their time
over the coming

and still I don't know
where my father
flying home
took a wrong turning

SUSANNE EHRHARDT (b. 1944)

I've Worked it Out

I've worked it out that when my parents parted
some time at the end of '43
I was about the size of a pea
eroding the lining of mum's womb.
He had been on compassionate leave
for grandfather's terminal illness, hence,
amid the stink of death that was Europe,
their chance to make life.

I know it like a memory, the walk to the station
with their arms hooked (that's how couples
walked those days), he in Luftwaffe uniform,
blue-grey, her favourite colour always,
she in the coat with the fox fur collar.
They talked of how it would be when it was over.
She saw the train out and walked back,
spent the rest of the pregnancy ducking bombs,
watching the city subside into rubble.

There was no news, but the letters stopped,
so he was listed missing. Someone claimed
to have seen him in Estonia, five hundred miles
from where he was last known to be.
She went to the fortune-teller who said
he'd be back in '51, or if not, by '53.
Later, she had him declared dead
for the sake of the war widow's pension.
All that time, I spooned the hated potato soup –
one for mummy, one for sister, one for granny,
three for father starving in the camp.

In '55, Adenauer negotiated the release
of the last POW's in Soviet hands.
Aged eleven, I watched her watch the trains go by.
Leaning from open wagons other men waved to us,
excited so soon after crossing the border.
It was then she gave up and wept.

VERA BRITTAIN (1893–1970)

···

The Lament of the Demobilised

'Four years,' some say consolingly. 'Oh well,
What's that? You're young. And then it must have been
A very fine experience for you!'
And they forget
How others stayed behind and just got on –
Got on the better since we were away.
And we came home and found
They had achieved, and men revered their names,
But never mentioned ours;
And no one talked heroics now, and we
Must just go back and start again once more.
'You threw four years into the melting-pot –
Did you indeed!' these others cry. 'Oh well,
The more fool you!'
And we're beginning to agree with them.

War Widow

I have grown old and dull, and out of date.
The children – but they are not children now –
They have run so fast that I am tired,
Left, like a runner who could not stay the course,
Lagging behind.

They don't remember you: they think they do.
They were too young to know you never shared
Their baby world: that your keen, questing mind
Had other fields to travel.

You are not old and dull and out of date!
You are the spare young soldier who looks down
From the tall picture, painted that last leave.
They look at you, and shrug, and their eyes say:
'He would have understood!'

I wonder . . . would you?

Had we grown old together,
I might have slid more gently into age;
You would have altered: touched by autumn's frost
To a more sober russet. As it is, you live
In the shrill green of youth, forever young,
As I last saw you – fifteen years today –
When you went back . . . to that:
And spring-time fled away.

Post-War Christmas

Lean forward Spring and touch these iron trees
And they will come to life!
Unchain the fettered stream, bring warmth to ease
The wounds of Winter's knife.
Lean forward Spring, and I will learn your art
Which out of love has grown.
(War, my life's Winter took my living heart,
And left a heart of stone.)
And though the bright drops on the holly tree
For ageless Christmas shine,
And though the world was saved through agony,
I faint through mine.
For he whose love once bore my grief away,
And made his joy my own,
Sleeps this cold Christmas in a colder clay,
And I must wake alone.
But if a new design for those who mourn
Is shaped through pain,
O Spring, lean forward with creative hands,
And hew this stone again!

The War Generation: Vale

We, whom the storm winds battered, come again
Like strangers to the places we have known,
Who sought men's understanding all in vain
For hardened hearts to grief's dark image grown;
So, passing through the careless crowd alone,
Ghosts of a time no future can restore,
We desolately roam for evermore
An empty shore.

For us they live till life itself shall end,
The frailties and the follies of those years,
Their strength which only pride of loss could lend,
Their vanished hopes, their sorrows and their tears;
But slowly towards the verge the dim sky clears,
For nobler men may yet redeem our clay
When we and war together, one wise day,
Have passed away.

MOTHERS

RUTH FAINLIGHT (b. 1931)

Handbag

My mother's old leather handbag,
crowded with letters she carried
all through the war. The smell
of my mother's handbag: mints
and lipstick and Coty powder.
The look of those letters, softened
and worn at the edges, opened,
read, and refolded so often.
Letters from my father. Odour
of leather and powder, which ever
since then has meant womanliness,
and love, and anguish, and war.

Columbines

Finding in a friend's garden columbines
It was as if they were those my mother grew,
And above all those coloured like a shell
Of rosy pearl seemed hers,
Returned, in all their freshness, from her garden
To remind me of, it should have been, happy days
When I was sheltered by her love and shared her flowers.
But by the vague bitter sorrow that arose
Out of the shadowy present of the past
I knew that it had not been so.
Wilful and unloving had been the daughter
My mother made, and all her flowers in vain
Offering of her life to mine.
What did I hope to find when I turned away from her
Towards a cold future, now my sum of years,
From the unprized only love earth had for me,
Demeter's for her lost Persephone?

Doorsteps

Cutting bread brings her hands back to me –
the left, with its thick wedding ring,
steadying the loaf. Small plump hands
before age shirred and speckled them.

She would slice not downwards but across
with an unserrated ivory-handled carving knife
bought from a shop in the Edgware Road,
an Aladdin's cave of cast-offs from good houses –
earls and countesses were hinted at.

She used it to pare to an elegant thinness.
First she smoothed already-softened butter
on the upturned face of the loaf. Always white,
Coburg shape. Finely rimmed with crust the soft
halfmoon half-slices came to the tea table
herringboned across a doylied plate.

I saw away at stoneground wholemeal.
Each slice falling forward into the crumbs
to be spread with butter's counterfeit
is as thick as three of hers. Doorsteps
she'd have called them. And those were white
in our street, rubbed with hearthstone
so that they glared in the sun
like new-dried tennis shoes.

Fanfare

*(for Winifrid Fanthorpe, born 5 February 1895,
died 13 November 1978)*

You, in the old photographs, are always
The one with the melancholy half-smile, the one
Who couldn't quite relax into the joke.

My extrovert dog of a father,
With his ragtime blazer and his swimming togs
Tucked like a swiss roll under his arm,
Strides in his youth towards us down some esplanade,

Happy as Larry. You, on his other arm,
Are anxious about the weather forecast,
His overdraft, or early closing day.

You were good at predicting failure: marriages
Turned out wrong because you said they would.
You knew the rotations of armistice and war,
Watched politicians' fates with gloomy approval.

All your life you lived in a minefield,
And were pleased, in a quiet way, when mines
Exploded. You never actually said
I told you so, but we could tell you meant it.

Crisis was your element. You kept your funny stories
Your music-hall songs for doodlebug and blitz-nights.
In the next cubicle, after a car-crash, I heard you
Amusing the nurses with your trench wit through the blood.

Magic alerted you. Green, knives and ladders
Will always scare me through your tabus.
Your nightmare was Christmas; so much organised
Compulsory whoopee to be got through.

You always had some stratagem for making
Happiness keep its distance. Disaster
Was what you planned for. You always
Had hoarded loaves or candles up your sleeve.

Houses crumbled around your ears, taps leaked,
Electric light bulbs went out all over England,
Because for you homes were only provisional,
Bivouacs on the stony mountain of living.

You were best at friendship with chars, gypsies,
Or very far-off foreigners. Well-meaning neighbours
Were dangerous because they lived near.

Me too you managed best at a distance. On the landline
From your dugout to mine, your nightly
Pass, friend was really often quite jovial.

You were the lonely figure in the doorway
Waving goodbye in the cold, going back to a sink-full
Of crockery dirtied by those you loved. We
Left you behind to deal with our crusts and gristle.

I know why you chose now to die. You foresaw
Us approaching the Delectable Mountains,
And didn't feel up to all the cheers and mafficking.

But how, dearest, will even you retain your
Special brand of hard-bitten stoicism
Among the halleluyas of the triumphant dead?

Crab Apple Jelly

Every year you said it wasn't worth the trouble –
you'd better things to do with your time –
and it made you furious when the jars
were sold at the church fête
for less than the cost of the sugar.

And every year you drove into the lanes
around Calverton to search
for the wild trees whose apples
looked as red and as sweet as cherries,
and tasted sharper than gooseberries.

You cooked them in the wide copper pan
Grandma brought with her from Wigan,
smashing them against the sides
with a long wooden spoon to split
the skins, straining the pulp

through an old muslin nappy.
It hung for days, tied with string
to the kitchen steps, dripping
into a bowl on the floor –
brown-stained, horrible,

a head in a bag, a pouch
of sourness, of all that went wrong
in that house of women. The last drops
you wrung out with your hands;
then, closing doors and windows

to shut out the clamouring wasps,
you boiled up the juice with sugar,
dribbling the syrup onto a cold plate
until it set to a glaze,
filling the heated jars.

When they were cool
you held one up to the light
to see if the jelly had cleared.
Oh, Mummy, it was as clear and shining
as stained glass and the colour of fire.

GRACE NICHOLS (b. 1950)

··

Like a Beacon

In London
every now and then
I get this craving
for my mother's food
I leave art galleries
in search of plantains
saltfish/sweet potatoes

I need this link

I need this touch
of home
swinging my bag
like a beacon
against the cold

Jugged Hare

She mourned the long-ears
Hung in the pantry, his shot fur
Softly dishevelled. She smoothed that,
Before gutting – yet she would rather
Sicken herself, than cheat my father
Of his jugged hare.

A tender lady, freakish as the creature –
But resolute. She peeled it to its tail.
Oh, fortitude! Her rings sparked in and out
Of newspaper wipes. Blood in a bowl,
Sacrificial gravy. A rarely afforded
Bottle of port.

She sustained marriage
On high events, as a child plays house.
Dramas, conciliations –
Today, the hare. She sent me out
To bury the skin,
Tossed the heart to the cat.

She was in full spate.

Fragrance of wine and herbs
Blessed our kitchen; like the hare's dessert
Of wild thyme; or like his thighs
As though braised by God. She smiled
And dished up on willow,
Having a nice touch in framing
One-off scenarios.

After the feast, my father was a lover
Deeply enhanced.
I heard them go to bed,
Kissing – still inside her picture.
Later, I heard her sob
And guessed it was the hare,
Troubled her. My father slept,
Stunned with tribute. She lay now
Outside her frame, in the hare's dark

Hating her marital skills
And her lady-hands, that could flense a hare
Because she wooed a man.
In years to come,
I understood.

CHARLOTTE MITCHELL

The Passing of the Telegram

I wanted to alert my phoneless daughter –
a student, on a grant –
that a later train than first advised
would contain an aged aunt.
The man at British Telecom was useless,
I put the phone down with a slam,
he said the only thing to do
was to send a gorillagram.

I had to send some furry ape
to Newcastle upon Tyne
to read the following message:
Aunt Win arriving sixteen forty-nine.

Home is the Hunter

She's watched for his return
at each day's evening, his briefcase
stuffed as if with deermeat,
umbrella a spent spear.
Forty years of triumphal entrances,
attentive welcomings, end in this
gift-loaded euphoric homecoming.
Something near to fear

stirs in her. The house
has been hers throughout the core
of every day, close shelter
for her busy morning hours,
her re-creative afternoons.
Now it opens its traitor door,
switches allegiance to his clamour,
his masterfulness, his more

insistent needs. How long had she
dug, hoed and planted the suburban
flower-patch, made it colourful
and fragrant for his weekend
leisure? Now he comes in with the air
of a pioneer, as if her patient garden
were wilderness for his first
cultivation; and she'll pretend

(habits are hard to break) when called on
to admire, that everything he grows
is magical, as if no million years
but he alone made this summer's rose.

Mating calls

WENDY COPE (b. 1945)

Giving Up Smoking

There's not a Shakespeare sonnet
Or a Beethoven quartet
That's easier to like than you
Or harder to forget.

You think that sounds extravagant?
I haven't finished yet –
I like you more than I would like
To have a cigarette.

Sonnet from the Portuguese

How do I love thee? Let me count the ways.
I love thee to the depth and breadth and height
My soul can reach, when feeling out of sight
For the ends of Being and ideal Grace.
I love thee to the level of everyday's
Most quiet need, by sun and candlelight.
I love thee freely, as men strive for Right;
I love thee purely, as they turn from Praise.
I love thee with the passion put to use
In my old griefs, and with my childhood's faith.
I love thee with a love I seemed to lose
With my lost saints, – I love thee with the breath,
Smiles, tears, of all my life! – and, if God choose,
I shall but love thee better after death.

A Birthday

My heart is like a singing bird
　　Whose nest is in a watered shoot:
My heart is like an apple-tree
　　Whose boughs are bent with thickset fruit;
My heart is like a rainbow shell
　　That paddles in a halcyon sea;
My heart is gladder than all these
　　Because my love is come to me.

Raise me a dais of silk and down;
　　Hang it with vair and purple dyes;
Carve it in doves and pomegranates,
　　And peacocks with a hundred eyes;
Work it in gold and silver grapes,
　　In leaves and silver fleurs-de-lys;
Because the birthday of my life
　　Is come, my love is come to me.

Box Room

First the welcoming. Smiles all round. A space
For handshakes. Then she put me in my place –
(Oh, with concern for my comfort). 'This room
Was always his – when he comes home
It's here for him. Unless of course,' she said,
'He brings a Friend,' She smiled 'I hope the bed
Is soft enough? He'll make do tonight
In the lounge on the put-u-up. All right
for a night or two. Once or twice before
He's slept there. It'll be fine I'm sure –
Next door if you want to wash your face.'
Leaving me 'peace to unpack' she goes. My weekend case
(Lightweight, glossy, made of some synthetic
Miracle) and I are left alone in her pathetic
Shrine to your lost boyhood. She must
Think she can brush off time with dust
From model aeroplanes. I laugh it off in self defence.
Who have come for a weekend to state my permanence.

Peace to unpack – but I found none
In this spare room which once contained you. (Dun-
Coloured walls, one small window which used to frame
Your old horizons.) What can I blame
For my unrest, insomnia? Persistent fear
Elbows me, embedded deeply here
In an outgrown bed. (Narrow, but no narrower
Than the single bed we sometimes share.)
On every side you grin gilt edged from long-discarded selves
(But where do I fit into the picture?) Your bookshelves
Are crowded with previous prizes, a selection
Of plots grown thin. Your egg collection
Shatters me – that now you have no interest
In. (You just took one from each, you never wrecked a nest,

You said.) Invited guest among abandoned objects, my position
Is precarious, closeted so – it's dark, your past a premonition
I can't close my eyes to. I shiver despite
The electric blanket and the deceptive mildness of the night.

AMY LOWELL (1874–1925)

The Taxi

When I go away from you
The world beats dead
Like a slackened drum.
I call out for you against the jutted stars
And shout into the ridges of the wind.
Streets coming fast,
One after the other,
Wedge you away from me,
And the lamps of the city prick my eyes
So that I can no longer see your face.
Why should I leave you,
To wound myself upon the sharp edges of the night?

Politeness

They walked awkwardly along the towpath
bumping together, because his arm
was round her shoulder. He was saying:
I shall always remember this walk.
I'll never forget last night.
I'll never forget you. Oh God.

After a pause, she made a short
non-committal noise. The morning had turned
wet and dark. She felt dilapidated by the rain
and of course had forgotten her umbrella
due to the unexpected turn of events.
Trust me, he said, *you will, won't you?*

Trust him to what, she wondered.
Which men could one trust? Any man
carrying a musical instrument, perhaps?
Any man walking along reading a book?
Most doctors – with reservations about those
wearing bow ties. *Trust you to what?* she asked.

To never let you down, he said,
splitting the infinitive, crushing her
against his wet tweeds. She fought
for breath as he loomed over her.
Little one, I can't let you go.
I'll be back on Thursday. Expect me.

So many imperatives. The situation
had become unwieldy. She longed
for buttered toast, looked furtively
at her watch. *I know, I know, we have*
so little time. The suffocating squeeze
into the spongy lapels.

I've never felt like this before
Have you ever felt like this before?
Fatigue and embarrassment were
all too familiar to her. She stirred the leaves
with the toe of her boot. *No* she said
politely. *Not exactly like this.*

PATRICIA BEER (b. 1924)

Mating Calls

It is not so much the song
Of the hump-backed whale, reaching
Through a hundred miles of sea
To his love that strikes us. We
Can be heard farther than he.

It is not the albatross
Either, with his strident voice
Promising the most tender
'Always' in tones of thunder.
Our vows may well go under.

Some kind of magpie keeps on
Singing, when his mate has gone,
Not only his notes but hers.
This moves us to pride and tears
That love should make us such bores.

POEMS ABOUT SEX

LYNN PETERS

I Suspect

I suspect
There would be more poems
About sex
If it rhymed with more than
Pecks
Necks
Erects and ejects.

This begins to sound promising.
I may write one.

Story of a Hotel Room

Thinking we were safe – insanity!
We went in to make love. All the same
Idiots to trust the little hotel bedroom.
Then in the gloom . . .
. . . And who does not know that pair of shutters
With the awkward hook on them
All screeching whispers? Very well then, in the gloom
We set about acquiring one another
Urgently! But on a temporary basis
Only as guests – just guests of one another's senses.

But idiots to feel so safe you hold back nothing
Because the bed of cold, electric linen
Happens to be illicit. . . .
To make love as well as that is ruinous.
Londoner, Parisian, someone should have warned us
That without permanent intentions
You have absolutely no protection
– If the act is clean, authentic, sumptuous,
The concurring deep love of the heart
Follows the naked work, profoundly moved by it.

Wild Nights – Wild Nights!
Were I with three
Wild Nights should be
Our luxury!

Futile – the Winds –
To a Heart in port –
Done with the Compass –
Done with the Chart!

Rowing in Eden –
Ah, the Sea!
Might I but moor – Tonight –
In Thee!

The Faithful Wife

I am away from home
A hundred miles from the blue curtains
I made at Christmas and the table
My grandfather brought back from Sorrento.
I am a career woman at a conference.
I love my husband. I value
Both what I own and what I do.

I left the forsythia half yellow,
The bluebells – lifted from a wood in Suffolk
Last year – still tight, the mint surfacing.
I must sweep the paths when I get back.

And here for the past week you and I
Have been conducting a non-affair
That could not even be called flirtation
That could not be called anything
Except unusually straightforward desire,
Adultery in the heart.
Life is so short.

The programme is ending.
11.30 – Conference disperses.
I watch everybody leaving.
It feels like grief, like the guillotine.

Your turn now; go home
With the 'Good-bye, love'
You use to every personable woman.

Get in your large car which ten years ago
Was full of sand and children's things
On summer evenings.
You are middle-aged now, as I am.
Write your notes up,
Fix the rattling window,
Keep your marriage vows. As I shall.

RUTH PITTER (b. 1897)

But for Lust

But for lust we could be friends,
    On each other's necks could weep:
In each other's arms could sleep
    In the calm the cradle lends:

Lends awhile, and takes away.
    But for hunger, but for fear,
Calm could be our day and year
    From the yellow to the grey:

From the gold to the grey hair,
    But for passion we could rest,
But for passion we could feast
    On compassion everywhere.

Even in this night I know
    By the awful living dead,
By this craving tear I shed,
    Somewhere, somewhere it is so.

Grease

Grease steals in like a lover
over the body of my oven.
Grease kisses the knobs
of my stove.
Grease plays with the small
hands of my spoons.
Grease caresses the skin
of my table-cloth,
Getting into my every crease.
Grease reassures me that life
is naturally sticky.

Grease is obviously having an affair with me.

The Hickie

I mouth
sorry in the mirror when I see
the mark I must have made just now
loving you.
Easy to say it's alright
adultery
like blasphemy is for believers but
even in our
situation simple etiquette says
love should leave us both unmarked.
You are on loan to me like a library book
and we both know it.
Fine if you love both of us
but neither of us must too much show it.

In my misted mirror
you trace two toothprints
on the skin of your shoulder and sure
you're almost quick enough
to smile out bright and clear for me
as if it was O.K.

Friends again, together in this bathroom
we finish washing love away.

Shoes

I don't know why I let you stay
But I just can't refuse
We have a smoke and right away
You're taking off your shoes

You haven't got a word to say
No gossip, jokes or news
I mention it's a rainy day
You're taking off your shoes

This isn't what you'd call romance
We tell no tender lies
I never even get a chance
To look into your eyes

The love we make is cold as death
It's not what I would choose
Before I even catch my breath
You're putting on your shoes

I wish that you would stay and eat
Or have a little talk
But you just knock me off my feet
And then you take a walk

Our crazy loving goes so fast
You've got no time to lose
I try to make the moment last
You're putting on your shoes

ALL OF THE LONELY ONES

FREDA DOWNIE (1929–93)

A Plain Girl

A plain girl moving simply enough
Until love turned her down flat,
Leaving her with her parents' lives to live
And trunk full of embroidered stuff.

She acknowledged her plainness thereafter,
Underlined it rigorously
With all the farm work she could find.
Forgot the knack of easy laughter.

Her sisters watched how her coarseness grew,
Saw time-killing work broaden her hands
And gait, watched her gather a man's strength
To herself in the only way that she knew.

Guardedly her brothers watched her come and go,
Kept an eye on her many distances
As though she were the unpredictable horse
They enclosed in the furthest meadow.

Her meagre words the family understood
And they never forgot to turn away
When, with a quiet ferocity,
She chopped unnecessary piles of wood.

Solitude

Laugh, and the world laughs with you,
   Weep, and you weep alone,
For sad old earth must borrow its mirth,
   But has trouble enough of its own.
Sing, and the hills will answer;
   Sigh, it is lost on the air,
The echoes bound to a joyful sound,
   But shrink from voicing care.

Rejoice, and men will seek you;
   Grieve, and they turn and go.
They want full measure of all your pleasure.
   But they do not need your woe.
Be glad, and your friends are many,
   Be sad, and you lose them all;
There are none to decline your nectared wine,
   But alone you must drink life's gall.

Feast, and your halls are crowded,
   Fast, and the world goes by.
Succeed and give – and it helps you live,
   But no man can help you die;
There is room in the halls of pleasure
   For a large and lordly train,
But one by one we must all file on
   Through the narrow aisles of pain.

Message

Pick up the phone before it is too late
And dial my number. There's no time to spare –
Love is already turning into hate
And very soon I'll start to look elsewhere.

Good, old-fashioned men like you are rare –
You want to get to know me at a rate
That's guaranteed to drive me to despair.
Pick up the phone before it is too late.

Well, wouldn't it be nice to consummate
Our friendship while we've still got teeth and hair?
Just bear in mind that you are forty-eight
And dial my number. There's no time to spare.

Another kamikaze love affair?
No chance. This time I'll have to learn to wait
But one more day is more than I can bear –
Love is already turning into hate.

Of course, my friends say I exaggerate
And dramatize a lot. That may be fair
But it is no fun being in this state
And very soon I'll start to look elsewhere.

I know you like me but I wouldn't dare
Ring you again. Instead I'll concentrate
On sending thought-waves through the London air
And, if they reach you, please don't hesitate –
Pick up the phone.

Valuable

(After reading two paragraphs in a newspaper)

All those illegitimate babies . . .
Oh girls, girls,
Silly little cheap things,
Why do you not put some value on yourselves,
Learn to say, No?
Did nobody teach you?
Nobody teaches anybody to say No nowadays,
People should teach people to say No.

O poor panther,
Oh your poor black animal,
At large for a few moments in a school for young children in Paris,
Now in your cage again,
How your great eyes bulge with bewilderment,
There is something there that accuses us,
In your angry and innocent eyes,
Something that says:
I am too valuable to be kept in a cage.

Oh these illegitimate babies!
Oh girls, girls,
Silly little valuable things,
You should have said, No, I am valuable,
And again, It is because I am valuable
I say, No.

Nobody teaches anybody they are valuable nowadays.

Girls, you are valuable,
And you, Panther, you are valuable,
But the girls say: I shall be alone
If I say 'I am valuable' and other people do not say it of me,
I shall be alone, there is no comfort there.

No, it is not comforting but it is valuable,
And if everybody says it in the end
It will be comforting. And for the panther too,
If everybody says he is valuable
It will be comforting for him.

VALERIE GILLIES (b. 1948)

Trick of Memory

Three years north
of the tropic of cancer
have changed me.
I no longer put oil on my head
or sew jasmine, to sleep with it in my hair.
I pinch shut the letters from India:
their language seems wrinkled
as the features of cholera.
It is difficult to picture their writer,
crosslegged on a teak swing indoors.

I used to long for a pair
of the silver toe-rings worn by women
married into the princely family.
Now their faint sound would seem
unattainable as a skein of geese.
I used to love the royal blue
of the two-tone sun-and-shade
silk sari worn by the mothers
of pretty boys named Dilip or Ajoy.
Now that blue would seem
remote as a piece of sky.
I do not care to remember
what husband might entitle me to toe-rings,
or what son would have sent me peacock saris.

Personals

Here in a magazine
Buy it and read
All of the lonely ones
Crying their need
Boy wanted, girl wanted
Man seeking friend
Who ever answers them?
How does it end?

They put their loneliness
Into an ad
Isn't it laughable?
Isn't it sad?
Boy wanted, girl wanted
Longing to meet
Old-fashioned, up-to-date
Clean and discreet

Over-worked investment broker
Planning to relax
Seeking sexy, blonde deduction
From his income tax
Convent-bred, confused young lady
Looking for a guide
Gentleman with private income
Hasn't any pride

Easy to laugh at them
That's understood
You've been the lucky one
You've got it good
Boy wanted, girl wanted
Man seeking friend
Who ever answers them?
How does it end?

AGAINST COUPLING

APHRA BEHN (1640–89)

A Letter to the Earl of Kildare, dissuading him from marrying Moll Howard

My Lord,
We pity such as are by tempest lost,
And those by Fortune's blind disposal crossed;
But when men see, and may the danger shun,
Yet headlong into certain ruin run:
To pity such, must needs be ridicule;
Do not (my Lord) be that unpitied fool.

There's a report, which round the Town is spread,
The famed Moll Howard you intend to wed;
If it be true, my Lord, then guard your head:
Horns, horns, by wholesale, will adorn your brows,
If e'er you make that rampant whore your spouse.
Think on the lewd debauches of her life;
Then tell me, if she's fit to be your wife.
She that to quench her lustful, hot desire,
Has kissed with dukes, lords, knights, and country squire;
Nay, grooms and footmen have been clawed off by her.

Whoring has all her life-time been her trade,
And D—set says, she is an exc'llent bawd:
But finding both will not defray expense,
She lately is become an evidence;
Swears against all that won't her lust supply,
And says, they're false as Hell to monarchy.

You had a wife; but, rest her soul, she's dead,
By whom your Lordship by the nose was led:
And will you run into that noose again,
To be the greatest monster among men?
Think on the horns that will adorn your head,
And the diseases that will fill your bed:
Pox upon pox, most horrid and most dire!
And ulcers filled with Hell's eternal fire.

Forbear therefore, and call your senses home;
Let reason love's blind passion overcome:
For, if you make this base report once true,
You'll wound your honour, purse, and body too.

FLEUR ADCOCK (b. 1934)

Against Coupling

I write in praise of the solitary act:
of not feeling a trespassing tongue
forced into one's mouth, one's breath
smothered, nipples crushed against the
ribcage, and that metallic tingling
in the chin set off by a certain odd nerve:

unpleasure. Just to avoid those eyes would help –
such eyes as a young girl draws life from,
listening to the vegetal
rustle within her, as his gaze
stirs polypal fronds in the obscure
sea-bed of her body, and her own eyes blur.

There is much to be said for abandoning
this no longer novel exercise –
for not 'participating in
a total experience' – when
one feels like the lady in Leeds who
has seen *The Sound of Music* eighty-six times;

or more, perhaps, like the school drama mistress
producing *A Midsummer Night's Dream*
for the seventh year running, with
yet another cast from 5B.
Pyramus and Thisbe are dead, but
the hole in the wall can still be troublesome.

I advise you, then, to embrace it without
encumbrance. No need to set the scene,
dress up (or undress), make speeches.
Five minutes of solitude are
enough – in the bath, or to fill
that gap between the Sunday papers and lunch.

THE OTHER SIDE OF THE STORY

CATHERINE LUCY CZERKAWSKA (b. 1950)

The Other Side of the Story

I am no pale princess out of fairy tale.
I would have my skin too thick to feel
The pea through my piled feather beds.
There is no prince charming enough
To dare my Rapunzel tower
Nor bring me a glass slipper
Nor weave me a rose encrusted bower.

But I will be malicious Morgan
Who wished fair Guinevere dead
Or Blodeuedd who was created flowers
And I will be the wicked queen
Who cuts off her suitors' heads
One by gory one,
Who carries fatal apples
And a poisoned spindle
And dances to her death
Beneath the blazing sun.

The Frog Prince

I am a frog
I live under a spell
I live at the bottom
Of a green well

And here I must wait
Until a maiden places me
On her royal pillow
And kisses me
In her father's palace.

The story is familiar
Everybody knows it well
But do other enchanted people feel as nervous
As I do? The stories do not tell,

Ask if they will be happier
When the changes come
As already they are fairly happy
In a frog's doom?

I have been a frog now
For a hundred years
And in all this time
I have not shed many tears,

I am happy, I like the life,
Can swim for many a mile
(When I have hopped to the river)
And am for ever agile.

And the quietness,
Yes, I like to be quiet
I am habituated
To a quiet life,

But always when I think these thoughts
As I sit in my well
Another thought comes to me and says:
It is part of the spell

To be happy
To work up contentment
To make much of being a frog
To fear disenchantment

Says, It will be *heavenly*
To be set free,
Cries, *Heavenly* the girl who disenchants
And the royal times, *heavenly*,
And I think it will be.

Come then, royal girl and royal times,
Come quickly,
I can be happy until you come
But I cannot be heavenly,
Only disenchanted people
Can be heavenly.

Not My Best Side

(Uccello: St George and the Dragon, *National Gallery)*

I

Not my best side, I'm afraid.
The artist didn't give me a chance to
Pose properly, and as you can see,
Poor chap, he had this obsession with
Triangles, so he left off two of my
Feet. I didn't comment at the time
(What, after all, are two feet
To a monster?) but afterwards
I was sorry for the bad publicity.
Why, I said to myself, should my conqueror
Be so ostentatiously beardless, and ride
A horse with a deformed neck and square hoofs?
Why should my victim be so
Unattractive as to be inedible,
And why should she have me literally
On a string? I don't mind dying
Ritually, since I always rise again,
But I should have liked a little more blood
To show they were taking me seriously.

II

It's hard for a girl to be sure if
She wants to be rescued. I mean, I quite
Took to the dragon. It's nice to be
Liked, if you know what I mean. He was
So nicely physical, with his claws
And lovely green skin, and that sexy tail,
And the way he looked at me,
He made me feel he was all ready to
Eat me. And any girl enjoys that.
So when this boy turned up, wearing machinery,

On a really *dangerous* horse, to be honest
I didn't much fancy him. I mean,
What was he like underneath the hardware?
He might have acne, blackheads or even
Bad breath for all I could tell, but the dragon –
Well, you could see all his equipment
At a glance. Still, what could I do?
The dragon got himself beaten by the boy,
And a girl's got to think of her future.

III

I have diplomas in Dragon
Management and Virgin Reclamation.
My horse is the latest model, with
Automatic transmission and built-in
Obsolescence. My spear is custom-built,
And my prototype armour
Still on the secret list. You can't
Do better than me at the moment.
I'm qualified and equipped to the
Eyebrow. So why be difficult?
Don't you want to be killed and/or rescued
In the most contemporary way? Don't
You want to carry out the roles
That sociology and myth have designed for you?
Don't you realise that, by being choosy,
You are endangering job prospects
In the spear- and horse-building industries?
What, in any case, does it matter what
You want? You're in my way.

A story wet as tears

Remember the princess who kissed the frog
so he became a prince? At first they danced
all weekend, toasted each other in the morning
with coffee, with champagne at night
and always with kisses. Perhaps it was
in bed after the first year had ground
around she noticed he had become cold
with her. She had to sleep
with heating pad and down comforter.
His manner grew increasingly chilly
and damp when she entered a room.
He spent his time in water sports,
hydroponics, working on his insect
collection.
        Then in the third year
when she said to him one day, my dearest,
are you taking your vitamins daily,
you look quite green, he leaped
away from her.
        Finally on their
fifth anniversary she confronted him.
'My precious, don't you love me any
more?' He replied, 'Rivet. Rivet.'
Though courtship turns frogs into princes,
marriage turns them quietly back.

SO MANY KINDS OF AWFUL MEN

FIONA PITT-KETHLEY (b. 1954)

Morning After

The morning after and there's little left
for either one of you to say.

There's nothing in his rooms. (The coffee that
he'd asked you back to have was never there.)
There's only time enough for him to drive
you into work – his place not yours.

He swears at every passing motorist
along the way, before he stops to put
you down. 'Last night,' he says, 'was . . . interesting.'

And you're left standing there. You notice then
he's dropped you far from where you'd meant to go.

Rondeau Redoublé

There are so many kinds of awful men –
One can't avoid them all. She often said
She'd never make the same mistake again:
She always made a new mistake instead.

The chinless type who made her feel ill-bred;
The practised charmer, less than charming when
He talked about the wife and kids and fled –
There are so many kinds of awful men.

The half-crazed hippy, deeply into Zen,
Whose cryptic homilies she came to dread;
The fervent youth who worshipped Tony Benn –
'One can't avoid them all,' she often said.

The ageing banker, rich and overfed,
Who held forth on the dollar and the yen –
Though there were many more mistakes ahead,
She'd never make the same mistake again.

The budding poet, scribbling in his den
Odes not to her but to his pussy, Fred;
The drunk who fell asleep at nine or ten –
She always made a new mistake instead.

And so the gambler was at least unwed
And didn't preach or sneer or wield a pen
Or hoard his wealth or take the Scotch to bed.
She'd lived and learned and lived and learned but then
There are so many kinds.

Yuppie Considering Life in Her Loft Apartment

Jeff is such a bastard.
Like I can't handle it.
All I did was throw the silver fork
he'd left stuck for a week
in the mud at the base
of my weeping willow tree
in the general direction of his chest
and while it was en route added,
'What am I, your maid, lunkhead?'
He, as usual, moved *before* the fork
crash landed on his bicep and said,
'No prob, no prob', and those were
his last words to me on his way
out of my orbit and into the
gravitational pull of some dumb broad.
Advice has been pouring in:
'One look and I told you –
he's a no-goodnik, but you said you
liked his shoes, so there's no point
talking to you is there?';
and, 'Cancel him offa yer floppy disk,
revise your memory bank
and write a new programme –
who needs the louse anyway?';
and, 'Join the club. Ya wanna
come with me for a facial? –
Elizabeth Arden have a special offer.'
The part that really gets to me
is that I forgot everything I learned
in that Psychology course I took last year:
'The Male Ego and How to Cope With It'.

The Apex

He was the apex of our triangle,
this we discovered, in the cluttered angle
of a chainstore changing room,
as I remarked on her perfume:
'Valkyrie?' I ventured. 'Yes, it's awful,
my boyfriend buys it, by the drawerful,
and he insists it smells just fine!'
'Oh yes!' I spluttered, 'so does mine!'

'Mini?' I murmured, for we had both selected
the same blue mini skirt, and both rejected
in similar material, a pair of jeans.
'My boyfriend likes me wearing them
as long as I don't talk to other men,
but they can stare, he thinks that's fine'
'That's funny' I said 'so does mine!'

So side by side, in the stark mirror, we compared
our looks, our shoes, our choice of clothes, our hair,
and realised that both of us had been obedient to the self
same whim and both of us were dressing just for him.

And as we surfaced from delusion,
we came as one to this conclusion,
that she was Monday, Wednesday, Friday,
and I was all the other days except for Sunday!
We looked into each other's eyes
and promised him a big surprise.

On Tuesday next, at half past eight,
unknown to him, a double date.
At Henry's wine bar on the Strand
we sat in state, a pint of shandy in each hand

and as we sat, we savoured it,
spicy sweat of unshaved armpit,
bliss of baggy dungarees
rolled up towards our freckled knees
and just enough designer stubble on our shins.
We both relaxed our double chins
and smiled, real smiles at the assembled company,
and were rewarded with a boyish grin
from weary worldly men drowning the day in gin,
who'd fed their youth to ravenous computers
and now, were last train possible commuters.

So occupied were we, and feeling so alive,
we did not notice him arrive.
We did not catch the shudder on his face,
the ripple of recoil in back and shoulder blades,
as he abruptly left the place.

I looked at her,
She looked at me.
We both dissolved in girlish glee
and drank to his departure long and deep,
and to the friendship we would keep
forever, for we both agreed
that though our choice had proved regrettable,
his taste in girlfriends was impeccable.

The Poet's Companion

Must be in mint condition, not disposed
To hayfever, headaches, hangovers, hysteria, these being
The Poet's prerogative.

Typing and shorthand desirable. Ability
To function on long walks and in fast trains an advantage.
Must be visible/invisible

At the drop of a dactyl. Should be either
A mobile dictionary, thesaurus and encyclopaedia,
Or have instant access to same.

Cordon bleu and accountancy skills essential,
Also cooking of figures and instant recall of names
Of once-met strangers.

Should keep a good address book. In public will lead
The laughter, applause, the unbearably moving silence.
Must sustain with grace

The role of Muse, with even more grace the existence
Of another eight or so, also camera's curious peeping
When the Poet is reading a particularly

Randy poem about her, or (worse) about someone else.
Ability to endure reproaches for forgetfulness, lack of interest,
Heart, is looked for,

Also instant invention of convincing excuses for what the Poet
Does not want to do, and long-term ability to remember
Precise detail of each.

Must be personable, not beautiful. The Poet
Is not expected to waste time supervising
The Companion. She will bear

Charming, enchanted children, all of them
Variations on the Poet theme, and
Impossibly gifted.

Must travel well, be fluent in the more aesthetic
European languages; must be a Finder
Of nasty scraps of paper

And the miscellany of junk the Poet loses
And needs *this minute, now*. Must be well-read,
Well-earthed, well able

To forget her childhood's grand trajectory,
And sustain with undiminished poise
That saddest dedication: *lastly my wife,*

Who did the typing.

Why Dorothy Wordsworth is not as Famous as her Brother

'I wandered lonely as a . . .
They're in the top drawer, William,
Under your socks –
I wandered lonely as a –
No not that drawer, the top one.
I wandered by myself –
Well wear the ones you can find,
No, don't get overwrought my dear,
I'm coming.'

'I was out one day wandering
Lonely as a cloud when –
Softboiled egg, yes my dear,
As usual, three minutes –
As a cloud when all of a sudden –
Look, I said I'll cook it,
Just hold on will you –
All right. I'm coming.

'One day I was out for a walk
When I saw this flock –
It can't be too hard, it had three minutes.
Well put some butter in it.
– This host of golden daffodils
As I was out for a stroll one –

'Oh you fancy a stroll, do you.
Yes, all right William. I'm coming.
It's on the peg. Under your hat.
I'll bring my pad, shall I, in case
You want to jot something down?'

Second Choice

Some men don't think affairs are worth the fares,
or even the price of a long-distance call –
say 20p cheap rate, out of peak hours –
to summon you to meet them.

A girl I know was dropped when her job went.
She worked close by but lived nearly an hour
away by train. Her man then reasoned I
might do – I'm near – just a mile's walk for him.
No need, of course, to ring me up before.

Last time he came, I hung around upstairs
and peeped between the attic banisters.
(I'd recognised his legs through our front door,
reflected in the mirror on the stairs.)

He knocked and knocked, ten minutes in the snow . . .

THEMES FOR WOMEN

LIZ LOCHHEAD (b. 1947)

Poem for My Sister

My little sister likes to try my shoes,
to strut in them,
admire her spindle-thin twelve-year-old legs
in this season's styles.
She says they fit her perfectly,
but wobbles
on their high heels, they're
hard to balance.

I like to watch my little sister
playing hopscotch, admire the neat hops-and-skips of her,
their quick peck,
never-missing their mark, not
over-stepping the line.
She is competent at peever.

I try to warn my little sister
about unsuitable shoes,
point out my own distorted feet, the callouses,
odd patches of hard skin.
I should not like to see her
in my shoes.
I wish she would stay
sure footed,
        sensibly shod.

Themes for Women

There is love to begin with, early love,
painful and unskilled, late love for matrons
who eye the beautiful buttocks and thick hair
of young men who do not even notice them.

Parturition, it figures, comes after, cataclysmic
at first, then dissolving into endless care
and rules and baths and orthodontic treatment,
Speech days, Open days, shut days, exams.

There are landscapes and inscapes too, sometimes tracts
of unknown counties, most often the one great hill
in low cloud, the waterfall, the empty sands, the few
snowdrops at the back door, the small birds flying.

Politics crop up at election time and ecology
any old time, no ocelot coats, no South African
oranges, a knowledge of the Serengeti
greater than the positioning of rubbish dumps
here in this off-shore island in hard times.

Seasons never go out of fashion, never will,
the coming of Spring, the dying fall
of Autumn into Winter, fine brash summers,
the red sun going down like a beach ball
into the sea. These do not escape the eyes
of women whose bodies obey the tides
and the cheese-paring sterile moon.

As you might expect, death hangs around a lot.
First ageing mothers, senile fathers; providing
the ham and sherry when the show is over,
examining stretched breasts to catch the process
of decay in time. In farmhouse kitchens they make

pigeon pies, weeping unexpectedly over
curved breasts among the floating feathers.
The men tread mud in after docking lambs' tails,
and smell of blood.

SELIMA HILL (b. 1945)

The Unsuccessful Wedding-Night

It's all because of Buster.
Of course, it's unreasonable,
he couldn't possibly have come –
his barking, his midnight walk,
the way he scratches at the blankets –

but as she presses her face
into the pillow of the small hotel,
she can't help missing him
terribly. She imagines the two of them
hiking in bright sunshine

over the Western Ghats; and soon
she begins to whimper to herself,
her runny nose trailing
over the foam pillows
like the Vasco da Gama of snails.

Convent

a fistful of notes
my heart

a thin must
covers the keyboard of ivory soldiers

girls are expected
to wear gloves

and a labour of love is lost
in plain sewing

each finger stitched
to the palm

the loose hem of the street
catches me

the tune
of a barrel organ

the monkey
playing alone

streetheart
no penny can buy it

I ought
to give my pocket

money for a poor child
going begging in the east

while the bell rings for angelus
here are gloves of silk a purse

on a string
worn over the shoulder

and nothing
in it

after prayers
there will be bread and butter soldiers

a measure of milk
plainsong

Thoughts After Ruskin

Women reminded him of lilies and roses.
Me they remind rather of blood and soap,
Armed with a warm rag, assaulting noses,
Ears, neck, mouth and all the secret places:

Armed with a sharp knife, cutting up liver,
Holding hearts to bleed under a running tap,
Gutting and stuffing, pickling and preserving,
Scalding, blanching, broiling, pulverising,
– All the terrible chemistry of their kitchens.

Their distant husbands lean across mahogany
And delicately manipulate the market,
While safe at home, the tender and the gentle
Are killing tiny mice, dead snap by the neck,
Asphyxiating flies, evicting spiders,
Scrubbing, scouring aloud, disturbing cupboards,
Committing things to dustbins, twisting, wringing,
Wrists red and knuckles white and fingers puckered,
Pulpy, tepid. Steering screaming cleaners
Around the snags of furniture, they straighten
And haul out sheets from under the incontinent
And heavy old, stoop to importunate young,
Tugging, folding, tucking, zipping, buttoning,
Spooning in food, encouraging excretion,
Mopping up vomit, stabbing cloth with needles,
Contorting wool around their knitting needles,
Creating snug and comfy on their needles.

Their huge hands! their everywhere eyes! their voices
Raised to convey across the hullabaloo,
Their massive thighs and breasts dispensing comfort,
Their bloody passages and hairy crannies,
Their wombs that pocket a man upside down!

And when all's over, off with overalls,
Quickly consulting clocks, they go upstairs,
Sit and sigh a little, brushing hair,
And somehow find, in mirrors, colours, odours,
Their essences of lilies and of roses.

ANNE STEVENSON (b. 1933)

The Marriage

They will fit, she thinks,
but only if her backbone
cuts exactly into his rib cage,
and only if his knees
dock exactly under her knees
and all four
agree on a common angle.

All would be well
if only
they could face each other.

Even as it is
there are compensations
for having to meet
nose to neck
chest to scapula
groin to rump
When they sleep.

They look, at least,
as if they were going
in the same direction.

The Message

The message of the men is linear.
Like rapid pines they swarm upwards
jostling for space
mutilating their roots in the race
sowing a shade so deep
within their conquered space
little else can grow
and *growth*, they are shouting, *growth*.

But the message of the women is love
has always been love.
It is the luminous shining
under the substance
opaque stickiness of pain and grief
greyness of wanting, heaviness of getting.

The saints knew it also
the wisemen, the incarnations of God
Christ, Buddha
brought it as an astonishing revelation.

But we were born knowing it.
It is the circle of light we carry
at the centre of our bodies
knowing, and forgetting
see with our eyes in visionary radiance
when we give birth
and lose and discover again
season after season
because we are orchard.

Safe Period

Your dry voice from the centre of the bed
asks 'Is it safe?'

and I answer for the days as if I owned them.
Practised at counting, I rock
the two halves of the month like a cradle.

The days slip over their stile
and expect nothing. They are just days,

and we're at it again, thwarting
souls from the bodies they crave.

They'd love to get into this room
under the yellow counterpane
we've torn to make a child's cuddly,

they'd love to slide into the sheets
between soft, much-washed
flannelette fleece,

they'd love to be here in the moulded spaces
between us, where there is no room,

but we don't let them. They fly about gustily,
noisy as our own children.

Soliloquy to a Belly

I have grown a belly.
It has swallowed up
my legs and arms,
even my head.

The government owns it.
The man
comes to examine it
regularly,
like the meter.
I say 'I am behind it',
but he has his union,
he has his schedule.

The old mothers
have come to my bedroom
to keep their vigil.
They sit and knit
straitjackets for daughters.
It's the species that matter,
it's all quite natural;
little husk,
you're for corn.

Along the street
the no-bellies walk.
In the space between
their breasts and legs
they've a squeeze
of desire, like picnic salt
in a twist of paper.
They'd like a belly
to sleep behind.

I'm afraid
my arms and legs
won't grow again.
It happens every day of the week,
you're not unique,
not even special.

I'll hem my sheets,
I'll let them read the meter twice,
I'll be nice to the midwife,
push when I'm told.
I'm lying in
behind this belly,
thin and cold.

Annunciation

It seems I must have been more fertile than most
to have taken that wind-blown
thistledown softly-spoken word
into my body and grown big-bellied with it.
Nor was I the first: there had been
rumours of such goings-on before my turn
came – tales of swansdown. Mine
had no wings or feathers actually
but it was hopeless trying to convince them.
They like to think it was a mystical
encounter, although they must know
I am not of that fibre – and to say I was
'troubled' is laughable.
What I do remember is a great rejoicing,
my body's arch and flow, the awe,
and the ringing and singing in my ears –
and then the world stopped for a little while.
But still they will keep on about the Word,
which is their name for it, even though I've
told them that is definitely
not how I would put it.
I should have known they'd try to take
possession of my ecstasy and
swaddle it in their portentous terminology.
I should have kept it hidden in the dark
web of my veins . . .
Though this child grows in me –
not unwanted certainly, but
not intended on my part; the risk
did not concern me at the time, naturally.
I must be simple to have told them anything.
Just because I stressed the miracle of it
they've rumoured it about the place that I'm

immaculate – but then they always were afraid
of female sexuality.
I've pondered these things lately in my mind.
If they should canonise me
(setting me up as chaste and meek and mild)
God only knows what nonsense
they'll visit on the child.

MARGE PIERCY (b. 1936)

The watch

At this moment hundreds of women
a few miles from here are looking
for the same sign of reprieve, the red
splash of freedom. We run to check,
squirming through rituals of If I don't
look till two o'clock, if I skip lunch,
if I am good, if I am truly sorry,
probing, poking, hallucinating changes.
Flower, red lily, scarlet petunia
bloom for me. And some lesser number
of women in other bedrooms and bathrooms
see that red banner unfurl and mourn!
Another month, another chance missed.
Forty years of our lives, that flag
is shown or not and our immediate
and sometimes final fate determined,
red as tulips, red as poppies satin,
red as taillights, red as a stoplight,
red as dying, our quick bright blood.

Night Feed

This is dawn.
Believe me
This is your season, little daughter.
The moment daisies open,
The hour mercurial rainwater
Makes a mirror for sparrows.
It's time we drowned our sorrows.

I tiptoe in.
I lift you up
Wriggling
In your rosy, zipped sleeper.
Yes, this is the hour
For the early bird and me
When finder is keeper.

I crook the bottle.
How you suckle!
This is the best I can be,
Housewife
To this nursery
Where you hold on,
Dear life.

A silt of milk
The last suck.
And now your eyes are open,
Birth-coloured and offended.
Earth wakes.
You go back to sleep.
The feed is ended.

Worms turn
Stars go in.
Even the moon is losing face.
Poplars stilt for dawn
And we begin
The long fall from grace.
I tuck you in.

Counting

You count the fingers first: it's traditional.
(You assume the doctor counted them too,
when he lifted up the slimy surprise
with its long dark pointed head and its father's nose
at 2.13 a.m. – 'Look at the clock!'
said Sister: 'Remember the time: 2.13.')

Next day the head's turned pink and round;
the nose is a blob. You fumble under the gown
your mother embroidered with a sprig of daisies,
as she embroidered your own Viyella gowns
when you were a baby. You fish out
curly triangular feet. You count the toes.

'There's just one little thing' says Sister:
'His ears – they don't quite match. One
has an extra whorl in it. No one will notice.'
You notice like mad. You keep on noticing.
Then you hear a rumour: a woman in the next ward
has had a stillbirth. Or was it something worse?

You lie there, bleeding gratefully.
You've won the Nobel Prize, and the VC,
and the State Lottery, and gone to heaven.
Feed-time comes. They bring your bundle –
the right one: it's him all right.
You count his eyelashes: the ideal number.

You take him home. He learns to walk.
From time to time you eye him,
nonchalantly, from each side.
He has an admirable nose.
No one ever notices his ears. No one
ever stands on both sides of him at once.

He grows up. He has beautiful children.

IN SUMMER

LOUISE GLÜCK

....

Flowering Plum

In spring from the black branches of the flowering plum tree
the woodthrush issues its routine
message of survival. Where does such happiness come from
as the neighbors' daughter reads into that singing,
and matches? All afternoon she sits
in the partial shade of the plum tree, as the mild wind
floods her immaculate lap with blossoms, greenish white
and white, leaving no mark, unlike
the fruit that will inscribe
unraveling dark stains in heavier winds, in summer.

Lilacs

Lilacs,
False blue,
White,
Purple,
Colour of lilac,
Your great puffs of flowers
Are everywhere in this my New England.
Among your heart-shaped leaves
Orange orioles hop like music-box birds and sing
Their little weak soft songs;
In the crooks of your branches
The bright eyes of song-sparrows sitting on spotted eggs
Peer restlessly through the light and shadow
Of all springs.
Lilacs in doorways
Holding quiet conversations with an early moon;
Lilacs watching a deserted house
Settling sideways into the grass of an old road;
Lilacs, wind-beaten, staggering under a lop-sided shock of bloom
Above a cellar dug into a hill.
You are everywhere.

The Arrival of the Bee Box

I ordered this, this clean wood box
Square as a chair and almost too heavy to lift.
I would say it was the coffin of a midget
Or a square baby
Were there not such a din in it.

The box is locked, it is dangerous.
I have to live with it overnight
And I can't keep away from it.
There are no windows, so I can't see what is in there.
There is only a little grid, no exit.

I put my eye to the grid.
It is dark, dark,
With the swarmy feeling of African hands
Minute and shrunk for export,
Black on black, angrily clambering.

How can I let them out?
It is the noise that appals me most of all,
The unintelligible syllables.
It is like a Roman mob,
Small, taken one by one, but by god, together!

I lay my ear to furious Latin.
I am not a Caesar.
I have simply ordered a box of maniacs.
They can be sent back.
They can die, I need feed them nothing, I am the owner.

I wonder how hungry they are.
I wonder if they would forget me
If I just undid the locks and stood back and turned into a tree.
There is the laburnum, its blond colonnades,
And the petticoats of the cherry.

They might ignore me immediately
In my moon suit and funeral veil.
I am no source of honey
So why should they turn on me?
Tomorrow I will be sweet God, I will set them free.

The box is only temporary.

ALICE MEYNELL (1847–1922)

....

The Rainy Summer

There's much afoot in heaven and earth this year;
   The winds hunt up the sun, hunt up the moon,
Trouble the dubious dawn, hasten the drear
   Height of a threatening noon.

No breath of boughs, no breath of leaves, of fronds,
   May linger or grow warm; the trees are loud;
The forest, rooted, tosses in her bonds,
   And strains against the cloud.

No scents may pause within the garden-fold;
   The rifled flowers are cold as ocean-shells;
Bees, humming in the storm, carry their cold
   Wild honey to cold cells.

August Afternoon

This is the hour
When all the babies
                are asleep.
Lulled by the drifting heat
                and sand,
Serenaded by the sea.
Pushed past in chariots
                like ancient Kings
They pass unconscious
Through the sunlit world,
The only shadows cast
By rocks upon the shore.
Their sleep is undisturbed
                by future days
And when they wake,
                they smile,
Vague memories of salty kisses,
                paddled toes
Are locked forever in their minds
As they are carried home.

Stopping Places

The long car journeys to the sea
must have their breaks, not always
in towns where there's no room
to park but at the pavement's edge,
in villages, or by the woods, or in lay-bys
vibrating to the passage of fast cars.
The seat's pushed forward, the boot's lifted,
the greaseproof paper
rustles encouragingly. The children
climb to the ground and posture about,
talk, clamber on gates, eat noisily.
They're herded back, the journey
continues.
    What do you think
they'll remember most of that holiday?
the beach? the stately home?
the hot kerb of the promenade?
No. It will often be those nameless places
where they stopped, perhaps for no more
than minutes. The rank grass
and the dingy robin by the overflowing
bin for waste, the gravel ridged by
numerous wheels and the briared wood
that no one else had bothered
to explore, the long inviting field
down which there wasn't time
to go – these will stick in their memories
when beauty spots evaporate.
Was it worth the expense?
                                but
these are the rewards of travelling.
There must be an end in sight
for the transient stopping places
to be necessary, to be memorable.

The Snake

A narrow fellow in the grass
Occasionally rides;
You may have met him, – did you not,
His notice sudden is.

The grass divides as with a comb,
A spotted shaft is seen;
And then it closes at your feet
And opens further on.

He likes a boggy acre,
A floor too cool for corn.
Yet when a child, and barefoot,
I more than once, at morn,

Have passed, I thought, a whip-lash
Unbraiding in the sun, –
When, stooping to secure it,
It wrinkled, and was gone.

Several of nature's people
I know, and they know me;
I feel for them a transport
Of cordiality;

But never met this fellow,
Attended or alone,
Without a tighter breathing,
And zero at the bone.

Sea-Horse

Holiday trophy from Cornwall
he lies in cotton wool, fingernail long.
Obsidian eye glitters.
He is light as a husk, fragile.
Embryo perfect
he seems not dead, but waiting.

My son weeps at his strangeness;
Pegasus and mermaids are more familiar.
Except in dreams we do not remember
his watery meadows,
the undulant winds of his prairie.
Is it accident we bring him here
to limestone hills?
Creatures of his kind rise patiently
age after age toward the air,
the spade fragments them,
we kick them up at every step.
Certainly, thrown out as junk,
he will become dust with them,
his particles will ride the fields in summer air
– a resurrection, briefly, into light.

The Grass so little has to do –
A Sphere of simple Green –
With only Butterflies to brood
And Bees to entertain –

And stir all day to pretty Tunes
The Breezes fetch along –
And hold the Sunshine in its lap
And bow to everything –

And thread the Dews, all night, like Pearls –
And make itself so fine
A Duchess were too common
For such a noticing –

And even when it dies – to pass
In Odors so divine –
Like Lowly spices, lain to sleep –
Of Spikenards, perishing –

And then, in Sovereign Barns to dwell –
And dream the Days away,
The Grass so little has to do
I wish I were a Hay –

Katydids

(Shore of Lake Michigan)

Katydids scraped in the dim trees,
And I thought they were little white skeletons
Playing the fiddle with a pair of finger-bones.

How long is it since Indians walked here,
Stealing along the sands with smooth feet?
How long is it since Indians died here
And the creeping sands scraped them bone from bone?
Dead Indians under the sands, playing their bones
　　against strings of wampum.
The roots of new, young trees have torn their graves
　　asunder,
But in the branches sit little white skeletons
Rasping a bitter death-dirge through the August
　　night.

THE WORLD AWRY

MAYA ANGELOU (b. 1928)

Televised

Televised news turns
a half-used day into
a waste of desolation.
If nothing wondrous preceded
the catastrophic announcements,
certainly nothing will follow, save
the sad-eyed faces of
bony children,
distended bellies making
mock at their starvation.
Why are they always
Black?
Whom do they await?
The lamb-chop flesh
reeks and cannot be
eaten. Even the
green peas roll on my plate
unmolested. Their innocence
matched by the helpless
hope in the children's faces.
Why do Black children
hope? Who will bring
them peas and lamb chops
and one more morning?

Penguin on the Beach

Stranger in his own element,
Sea-casualty, the castaway manikin
Waddles in his tailored coat-tails. Oil

Has spread a deep commercial stain
Over his downy shirtfront. Sleazy, grey,
It clogs the sleekness. Far too well

He must recall the past, to be so cautious:
Watch him step into the waves. He shudders
Under the froth, slides, slips, on the wet sand,

Escaping to dryness, dearth, in a white cascade,
An involuntary shouldering off of gleam.
Hands push him back into the sea. He stands

In pained and silent expostulation.
Once he knew a sunlit, leaping smoothness,
But close within his head's small knoll, and dark

He retains the image: oil on sea,
Green slicks, black lassos of sludge
Sleaving the breakers in a stain-spread scarf.

He shudders now from the clean flinching wave,
Turns and plods back up the yellow sand,
Ineffably weary, triumphantly sad.

He is immensely wise: he trusts nobody. His senses
Are clogged with experience. He eats
Fish from his Saviour's hands, and it tastes black.

Strontium 90

How can it be
That this rambling river,
This hill–clasped village
Gave you your name?
Just now splashed with the brilliance of broom
Deep in a dream of bluebells,
Heady with scent of hawthorn.

Yet, climb out of this valley a little
And it becomes more possible.
These stark mountains,
Hard outlines on the sky,
Turbulent outcrop of rock
Cloud grey, moonscaped,
The harsh heather, dark,
Lacking all promise of purple
The rubble-rounded holes,
Gashed ground,
This miner's ruined home;
A single rowan tree
Planted to ward off evil
Now marks the spot.

Here no bird sings.

May Day, 1986

(for Tadeusz Sławek)

Yesterday, the weather in Warsaw
was the same as London's: 'sunny; 18°'
(sixty-four Fahrenheit). I am sitting
in a walled garden drinking gin,
the fading sky as blue as this tonic water
loosening its bubbles against the flat ice.

What is in the air? The first midges;
a television three doors down, its hum
like this lone bat avoiding the walnut tree.
A dog barks. In other houses lights come on –
the street an Advent Calendar opening
its doors. This house is in darkness,

its seven windows admitting the night.
I'm trying to read *Mansfield Park*, to learn
how Fanny finds love and a mansion
through keeping silence. All week
the weather report has plotted the wind
leaving Chernobyl with its freight

of fall-out: cancer settling on Poland –
the radioactivity an inaudible fizz
in the cells, rupturing thorax or liver,
the intimacy of the bowel. They say it won't
reach here. I stare at the sky till all
I can see are the dead cells of my eyes,

jumping and falling. It's too dark to read –
only the flare of a late *Kerria japonica*,
trained to the wall. I think of your letter
in my drawer with the handkerchiefs,
one page torn by an earlier reader. Socrates
distrusted writing, its distance from

the grain of the voice. I come indoors
to write you all the things I couldn't say
a year ago. Later, on the news, they will show
gallons of contaminated Polish milk
swilled into sewage, a boy crying
at the sting of iodine he must swallow

against the uncertain air.

DILYS ROSE (b. 1954)

Dream Feast

Like pie-dogs, they cower at the tail end
of every interminable queue, alert to nothing
but the sudden movement of a foot. They pick
and scratch at the periphery, unseeing,
distractedly drawing uncertain circles in the dirt.
They're etched on the scenery. They'll not desert
for richer dunghills but spend a lifetime
praying for windfalls, rotting morsels.
The last lean moon convinced them
they'd be mad to stray. So they linger,
the ugly unlovable glut of dull-eyed waifs
clutching the filthy hem of the world's skirt.

They sleep a lot: their dreams are crammed
with sides of beef, mountains of rice.

THE BEGINNING OF AUTUMN

MARGE PIERCY (b. 1936)

The matrimonial bed

That first winter in the middle
of the night you could not sleep
and woke me because the caress
of my unconscious breath across
your outflung knuckle roused you.
I opened my eyes to your cheek
cradled on my thigh.
                  You bear
the same name and wear
the same face, man who pretends
deep breathing gusty sleep
beside me as vainly I rub
my breasts against your back
curved away like the shell of a turtle.

Song at the Beginning of Autumn

Now watch this autumn that arrives
In smells. All looks like summer still;
Colours are quite unchanged, the air
On green and white serenely thrives.
Heavy the trees with growth and full
The fields. Flowers flourish everywhere.

Proust who collected time within
A child's cake would understand
The ambiguity of this –
Summer still raging while a thin
Column of smoke stirs from the land
Proving that autumn gropes for us.

But every season is a kind
Of rich nostalgia. We give names –
Autumn and summer, winter, spring –
As though to unfasten from the mind
Our moods and give them outward forms.
We want the certain, solid thing.

But I am carried back against
My will into a childhood where
Autumn is bonfires, marbles, smoke;
I lean against my window fenced
From evocations in the air.
When I said autumn, autumn broke.

Sonnet XXXI

Oh, oh, you will be sorry for that word!
Give back my book and take my kiss instead.
Was it my enemy or my friend I heard,
'What a big book for such a little head!'
Come, I will show you now my newest hat,
And you may watch me purse my mouth and prink!
Oh, I shall love you still, and all of that.
I never again shall tell you what I think.
I shall be sweet and crafty, soft and sly;
You will not catch me reading any more:
I shall be called a wife to pattern by;
And some day when you knock and push the door,
Some sane day, not too bright and not too stormy,
I shall be gone, and you may whistle for me.

Autumn — Almost

Autumn almost
and earth about to turn another way,
her magic circles of light and life fulfilled.

Now the strange heaviness begins to settle,
soon the rains will come and a scent of dampness
clinging to your coat and hair.

When you come you are warm and dark,
my seasons change,
you bring with you the mystery
of early fallen leaves
and a bright sky heavy with snow.

Let me wind you in the turning of my seasons,
let me spin a wild web,
cover you with early autumn whisperings
and then let the earth turn her winds around,
bearing our love towards spring.

The Tired Man

I am a quiet gentleman,
   And I would sit and dream;
But my wife is on the hillside,
   Wild as a hill-stream.

I am a quiet gentleman,
   And I would sit and think;
But my wife is walking the whirlwind
   Through night as black as ink.

O, give me a woman of my race
   As well controlled as I,
And let us sit by the fire,
   Patient till we die!

What's that smell in the kitchen?

All over America women are burning dinners.
It's lambchops in Peoria; it's haddock
in Providence; it's steak in Chicago;
tofu delight in Big Sur; red
rice and beans in Dallas.
All over America women are burning
food they're supposed to bring with calico
smile on platters glittering like wax.
Anger sputters in her brainpan, confined
but spewing out missiles of hot fat.
Carbonized despair presses like a clinker
from a barbecue against the back of her eyes.
If she wants to grill anything, it's
her husband spitted over a slow fire.
If she wants to serve him anything
it's a dead rat with a bomb in its belly
ticking like the heart of an insomniac.
Her life is cooked and digested,
nothing but leftovers in Tupperware.
Look, she says, once I was roast duck
on your platter with parsley but now I am Spam.
Burning dinner is not incompetence but war.

Song of the Woman Past Forty

Just rough me a scourging exfoliating scrub.
Rigour me a vigorous cellulite rub.
Tone me. Cleanse me. May the tingle of astringent
dewy-freshen cheeks till they glow refulgent.
With whipped creme anoint me.
With face mask appoint me
born again woman, resculptured, resplendent.

Oh let me not lapse into a Brooknered malaise,
but sing me a song of japonica'd days
Dior me. Lauder me. May rejuvenating scents
burn holes in my purse and my too common sense.
Let liposomes unwrinkle me
and neosomes retwinkle me –
I, who was ravaged by my cold-cream innocence.

And give me the gall to dye my greying roots
or waste all my wage in a blow-out at Boots.
'Try me', 'Test me', woo concoctions I select
from the alchemists' trove that defies intellect.
May wild claims come true
and the phoenix rise new
from the ashes of fictions – the words that have wrecked.

Getting Older

The first surprise: I like it.
Whatever happens now, some things
that used to terrify have not:

I didn't die young, for instance. Or lose
my only love. My three children
never had to run away from anyone.

Don't tell me this gratitude is complacent.
We all approach the edge of the same blackness
which for me is silent.

Knowing as much sharpens
my delight in January freesia,
hot coffee, winter sunlight. So we say

as we lie close on some gentle occasion:
every day won from such
darkness is a celebration.

DESANKA MAKSIMOVIĆ (b. 1898)

TRANSLATED BY VASA D. MIHAILOVICH

For Lies Spoken out of Kindness

I seek mercy
for those who lack the courage
to tell the evil one that he is evil
or the bad one that he is bad,
for those who hesitate
to hurt with the truth,
for the people who lie out of kindness.
For the man who would rather be humiliated
than humiliate,
for the man who has no heart
to pull down a mask when he sees it
on someone's face,
for people who cannot insult
those of different thoughts and creeds,
for those who never could
pronounce a sentence to others,
for whom all judges seem strict,
for every kind untruthful story
and other similar weaknesses.

from *Goblin Market*

Morning and evening
Maids heard the goblins cry:
'Come buy our orchard fruits,
Come buy, come buy:
Apples and quinces,
Lemons and oranges,
Plump unpecked cherries,
Melons and raspberries,
Bloom-down-cheeked peaches,
Swart-headed mulberries,
Wild free-born cranberries,
Crab-apples, dewberries,
Pine-apples, blackberries,
Apricots, strawberries; –
All ripe together
In summer weather, –
Morns that pass by,
Fair eves that fly;
Come buy, come buy:
Our grapes fresh from the vine,
Pomegranates full and fine,
Dates and sharp bullaces,
Rare pears and greengages,
Damsons and bilberries,
Taste them and try:
Currants and gooseberries,
Bright-fire-like barberries,
Figs to fill your mouth,
Citrons from the South,
Sweet to tongue and sound to eye;
Come buy, come buy.'

DENISE LEVERTOV (b. 1923)

Idyll

The neighbor's Black Labrador, his owners
out at work, unconscious anyone
is watching him, rises again and again
on hind legs to bend with his paws
the figtree's curving branches
and reach the sweet figs with his black lips.

MURIEL STUART (1885–1967)

The Seed-Shop

Here in a quiet and dusty room they lie,
    Faded as crumbled stone or shifting sand,
Forlorn as ashes, shrivelled, scentless, dry –
    Meadows and gardens running through my hand.

In this brown husk a dale of hawthorn dreams;
    A cedar in this narrow cell is thrust
That will drink deeply of a century's streams;
    These lilies shall make summer on my dust.

Here in their safe and simple house of death,
    Sealed in their shells, a million roses leap;
Here I can blow a garden with my breath,
    And in my hand a forest lies asleep.

Return Visit

This time I see there's grey dust
on the lamp,
notice an off-white tablecloth.
The waiters seem less gay than camp;
I check inflated prices
on their broken bric-a-brac.

But is it still the same,
this crazy cafe in a narrow street?
Maybe we've changed,
have disobeyed
like Lot's wife looking back.

The sea wind licks our lips
with salt again;
helpless we turn to see
our love dissolving in the rain.

JEAN EARLE (b. 1909)

Menopause

Now and again –
Since I was quite young –
I reckon my quota of seed
That we stopped from growing: not, of course,
All would have made it – there wasn't time
Nor strength in myself. But I think of them.

We raised three — and couldn't really have done
With more. It just feels strange
I might have had a dozen
Persons in my gift: and who would they have been?

In school biology, we were told once
How the female seeds
Are laid down at her making; one to go
Every month, when her body's ready,
Taking its chance.

I remember sniggers — also, myself
Looking from the window
Even as I smirked. What a day it was,
Blue and white . . .
And the thing seemed wonderful?

Seed by seed, lined up for years,
Waiting in my dark for the blind push
To be someone. More curious to me
Than the well-known puzzles,
Everyone's go. God — the stars . . .

I don't suppose Jack ever gave a thought
To such ideas. Men are so wasteful,
Careless of their seed. I often guess
What lives those might have had
Given some luck.

The colours of their eyes . . .

Golden Bough

These lovely groves of fountain-trees that shake
A burning spray against autumnal cool
Descend again in molten drops to make
The rutted path a river and a pool.

They rise in silence, fall in quietude,
Lie still as looking-glass to every sense
Save where their lion-colour in the wood
Roars to miraculous heat and turbulence.

EMILY DICKINSON (1830–86)

Autumn

The morns are meeker than they were,
The nuts are getting brown;
The berry's cheek is plumper,
The rose is out of town.

The maple wears a gayer scarf,
The field a scarlet gown.
Lest I should be old-fashioned,
I'll put a trinket on.

The Other Woman

The other woman
lies
between us like a bolster.
When I hit out wild she's
insubstantial a
flurry of feathers a mere
sneezing irritant.
When my shaped and hardened words turn
machine-gun
against you she's rock solid
the sandbag you hide behind.

The other woman
lies
when she says she does not want
your guts for her garterbelt.
I send out spies, they say relax
she's a hag she's just a kid
she's not a patch she's nothing to she's
no oil painting.
I'd know her anywhere.
I look for her in department stores, I scan
every cinema-queue.
Sometimes suddenly in some downtown restaurant
I catch her eye
casting crazily around for me.

The other woman
lies
the other side of my very own mirror.
Sweet, when I smile
straight out for you, she
puts a little twist on it, my
right hand never knows what her left is doing.
She's sinister.
She does not mean you well.

It Sounds Like Autumn

It sounds like autumn
the pain of leaves
turning grass turning
over in their morning
sleep waking later
than they did
the day before.
It sounds like autumn
crispness hissing
in the dew
the birdsong gone
fragile overnight.
My room is filled
with cold still air
and yesterday's plumpness
has turned to bone again
as I sit staring
at the hard floor
the purple floor
carpet the colour
of burnt heather.

Traitor

We were from the beginning close partners,
worked well together,
saw eye to eye.
He went out, brought in material, made the contacts:
I had the ideas, laid down policy,
was, I thought, the dominant element,
tactfully now and then letting him think he had control.
    At first I made excuses,
pretended not to notice,
overlooked the small rebellions
ignored the subtle underminings
until the truth was unavoidable.
    We do not face each other across a table of deadlocked
negotiations:
the relationship is sidelong.
I do not admit,
he does not assert,
that he is boss
and will some day apply
the final ineluctable sanction.

Sometimes

Sometimes things don't go, after all,
from bad to worse. Some years, muscadel
faces down frost; green thrives; the crops don't fail,
sometimes a man aims high, and all goes well.

A people sometimes will step back from war;
elect an honest man; decide they care
enough, that they can't leave some stranger poor.
Some men become what they were born for.

Sometimes our best efforts do not go·
amiss; sometimes we do as we meant to.
The sun will sometimes melt a field of sorrow
that seemed hard frozen: may it happen for you.

Stretch Marks

Lying awake in a provincial town
I think about poets. They are mostly
men, or Irish, turn out old yellow
photographs, may use four letter words,
stick pigs or marry twice, and edit
most of the books and magazines.

Most poets, who are men, and get to
the bar first at poetry readings,
don't like us fey or even feminist,
too old, too young, or too intense,
and monthlies to them are just the
times when very few need us.

Gowned like women in funereal black
they have friends who went punting
on the Cam. I'm not too clear
what others did in Oxford, except
avoid the traffic, bathe in fountains,
drunkenly, a different shade of blue.

Mostly they teach, and some must be
fathers, but they have no stretch marks
on their smooth stomachs to prove it.
At least we know our children
are our own. They can never really
tell, but poems they can be sure of.

Urban Lyric

The gaunt lady of the service wash
stands on the threshold and blinks in the sunlight.

Her face is yellow in its frizz of hair
and yet she smiles as if she were fortunate.

She listens to the hum of cars passing
as if she were on a country lane in summer,

or as if the tall trees edging this
busy street scattered blessings on her.

Last month they cut a cancer out of her throat.
This morning she tastes sunshine in the dusty air.

And she is made alert to the day's beauty,
as if her terror had wakened poetry.

When You Move Out

LIZ LOCHHEAD (b. 1947)

The Empty Song

Today saw the last of my Spanish shampoo.
Lasted an age now that sharing with you,
such a thing of the past is.
Giant Size. The brand
was always a compromise.
My new one's tailored exactly to my needs.
Nonspill. Protein-rich.
Feeds Body, promises to solve my problem hair.
Sweetheart, these days it's hard to care,
But oh oh insomniac moonlight
how unhoneyed is my middle of the night.
I could see you
far enough. Beyond me
how we'll get back together.
Campsites in Spain, moonlight,
heavy weather.
Today saw the end of my Spanish shampoo,
the end of my third month without you.

After a Warrant Sale

I watched her go,
Ann-next-door
(dry-eyed,
as dignified
as could be expected)
the day after they came,
sheriff's men
with the politeness of strangers
impersonally
to rip her home apart –
to tear her life along the dotted line
officially.

On the sideboard that went for fifteen bob,
a photograph.
Wedding-day Walter and
Ann: her hair was lightened,
and her heart.
No-one really knows
when it began to show –
trouble, dark roots.

It was common knowledge
there were faults on both sides,
and the blame –
whether it was over drink
or debt no-one seems to know,
or what was owing to exactly whom.
Just in the end the warrant sale,
and Ann's leaving.

But what seemed strange:
I wondered why,
having stayed long past the death of love
and the ashes of hope,
why pack it up and go
over some sticks of furniture
and the loss of one's only partially
paid-for washing machine?

Those who are older tell me,
after a married year or two
the comforts start to matter
more than the comforting.
But I am very young,
expecting not too much of love –
just that it should completely solve me.
And I can't understand.

LIZ LOCHHEAD (b. 1947)

Fin

I know it's the end.
I can see it coming. I'm
like those women in the cinema who make you mad
fumbling for gloves
elbowing themselves into coats, buttoning up –
such a final snapping shut of handbags
the minute it looks like it's all over
but a change of mood and music.
So you demand response, do you,
right to the bitter end, you like
to see the credits roll?
I'm off.

When You Move Out
from 'From Other Lovers'

You mark each box with a thick black pen.
You will always be neat, no matter what's said.
And fair. You do not pack what is not yours.
Even the joint presents: the Chinese vase,
the white dinner plates, the samovar,
you leave to her. You won't miss things.

At night you will lie on a different side.
Listen to another station to send you to sleep.
You will never play Nina Simone, again.
Other things won't be possible. Restaurants,
parks, cinemas, pubs. Avoid them. They are dangerous.
Never go near another garden. There's no point,

growing peonies to blossom without you. Delphiniums.
Take up something else. *It doesn't matter what.*

Division

'We are separated'
I hear myself say to well-meaning people.
As if we were curd and whey
or some referee had parted us two
wrestlers sparring in the ring of life.
As if we were milk and cream
or some great ocean, forged by God's wrathful hand,
instantly divided us, for Eternity.

'We are separated'
I say, and well-meaning people reply
'Oh, I'm sorry, I didn't know.'
Perhaps this news should be scooped on the front page,
or levered in a coffin, and sent ceremoniously
to the graveyard of wrecked marriages
where the taboo of grief can fester.

'We are two'
I want to say, head held high.
We were never
   Two hearts beating as one
   Two souls united in Heaven's match
   Two halves made whole.
Never that, I can say, with no bitterness.
We sparked together, but smouldered intact.
Out chidren are the blood link.
That is all.

One Art

The art of losing isn't hard to master;
so many things seem filled with the intent
to be lost that their loss is no disaster.

Lose something every day. Accept the fluster
of lost door keys, the hour badly spent.
The art of losing isn't hard to master.

Then practice losing farther, losing faster:
places, and names, and where it was you meant
to travel. None of these will bring disaster.

I lost my mother's watch. And look! my last, or
next-to-last, of three loved houses went.
The art of losing isn't hard to master.

I lost two cities, lovely ones. And, vaster,
some realms I owned, two rivers, a continent.
I miss them, but it wasn't a disaster.

– Even losing you (the joking voice, a gesture
I love) I shan't have lied. It's evident
the art of losing's not too hard to master
though it may look like (*Write* it!) like disaster.

A Letter

Your handwriting. A letterbomb
potentially. Blank side upmost on my mat
to turn it over was to trigger what
could blow my pieced-together calm.

In day thoughts a grey ghost.
Livid in dreams. Damn you, I'm not blind
to the shock of your writing, its cockeyed slant, my mind
flips blank side uppermost.

What can you possibly want to say?
It fell so quietly I did not hear it drop.
White and flat and foreign, the envelope
does not give anything away.

Once letters flew like birds
between us. I'd read and read again, stuff
your spilling pages behind every clock and photograph.
They were full of everything but words.

This'll be the usual. The job's still fine,
I suppose? You'll ask me how are John and Di,
has Doreen had her baby, how am I
how's he and this new life of mine?

You talk of your new loves. Plural. Wild oats
at your age. Jesus, you should know better.
I'm mad at my own tears, but not enough to rip this letter.
Recently I've burnt nothing but my boats.

Though I confess that bitter confetti of the last one.
But that was in passion – these days it's far too late
for anything except to (eventually) reply to it –
the past that isn't dead enough to stuff a cushion.

The Lines are Down
(To D.C.)

I can't believe you've gone,
still, after all this time,
I read a poem,
see a play,
hear music that you'd like
and want to phone you,
hear your swift response.

I did that once –
heard shrill ringing
echoing through empty rooms.

Now I know
your number's disconnected,
dead.
My fingers hesitate,
what would I say
if you should answer me?

The gap between us now
is far too wide
for trivial chat;
your traveller's tales
too strange for telephones.

And I'm afraid
that you might call me back.

LIZ LOCHHEAD (b. 1947)

How Have I Been

since you last saw me?
Well,
      I've never been lonely
      I've danced at parties,
      and drunk flat beer
with other men;
      I've been to the cinema and seen
      one or two films you would have liked
with other men;
      I've passed the time in amusement arcades
      and had one or two pretty fruitless
      goes on the fruit machine;
      I've memorised the patterns
      of miscellaneous neckties.
Indifferent, I
      put varying amounts of sugar
in different coffee cups
      and adjusted myself to divers heights
      of assorted goodnight kisses, but
my breasts (once bitten)
      shy away from contact
I keep   a curb
      on mind and body –
Love?   I'm no longer
        exposing myself.

FRIENDSHIP

ELIZABETH JENNINGS (b. 1926)

Friendship

Such love I cannot analyse;
It does not rest in lips or eyes,
Neither in kisses or caress.
Partly, I know, it's gentleness

And understanding in one word
Or in brief letters. It's preserved
By trust and by respect and awe.
These are the words I'm feeling for.

Two people, yes, two lasting friends.
The giving comes, the taking ends.
There is no measure for such things.
For this all Nature slows and sings.

For Eileen

You said
'I like the shape of our friendship'.
True, it had a definite beginning.
The accidental meeting at the formal luncheon
Was instant joyful connection.
We were the last to leave. Drunk at 4 p.m.,
You thanked our host for coming.

But its beginning, like its end, was out of character.
For the most part it was a married female friendship
Conducted Monday to Friday, nine to five.
No all nighters.
No no-holds-barred drunken confidences.
No weekends.
Married female friendship –
An art form, bred of constrictions
Which are the stuff of it.
Fitted in the spaces between the children.
Half sentences thrown across the noise of playing
Or fighting.
Patrick kicked me.
I want the doll's pram.
Clara's cut herself – there's *blood*.
I want a biscuit.
Anyway, it's time to go.
The men are coming home.

Was it death that did it.
Gave the friendship its shape.
Hot-housed it.
Gave it the lovers' mode
Of precious, planned-for time
Stolen from children, men, work.

Long journeys for brief meetings
Rich with significance.
Mutual, pleasurable self-analysis when you said,
'I like the shape of our friendship'.

EMILY DICKINSON (1830–86)

....

Alter? When the hills do.
Falter? When the sun
Question if his glory
Be the perfect one.

Surfeit? When the daffodil
Doth of the dew:
Even as herself, O friend!
I will of you!

THE OLD FOLK

RACHEL FIELD

Something Told the Wild Geese

Something told the wild geese
   It was time to go.
Though the fields lay golden
   Something whispered, 'Snow.'

Leaves were green and stirring,
   Berries, lustre-glossed,
But beneath warm feathers
   Something cautioned, 'Frost.'

All the sagging orchards
   Steamed with amber spice,
But each wild breast stiffened
   At remembered ice.

Something told the wild geese
   It was time to fly –
Summer sun was on their wings,
   Winter in their cry.

Bitter for Sweet

Summer is gone with all its roses,
    Its sun and perfumes and sweet flowers,
    Its warm air and refreshing showers:
        And even Autumn closes.

Yea, Autumn's chilly self is going,
    And Winter comes which is yet colder;
    Each day the hoar-frost waxes bolder,
        And the last buds cease blowing.

Let No Charitable Hope

Now let no charitable hope
Confuse my mind with images
Of eagle and of antelope:
I am in nature none of these.

I was, being human, born alone;
I am, being woman, hard beset;
I live by squeezing from a stone
The little nourishment I get.

In masks outrageous and austere
The years go by in single file;
But none has merited my fear,
And none has quite escaped my smile.

Her Retirement

Just a little party, nothing swank,
I told the founder, but you know Mr B.
There are so many of you here to thank.

I leave you the later tube trains, dank
At the hand-rails from a human sea,
Dreaming down to Morden via Bank.

I've homed quietly to port while others sank,
By keeping at my stenography.
There are so many of you here to thank.

I scan the backs of houses, rank on rank:
The comfy lamps, the oblique misery
Streaming down to Morden via Bank.

Our gardens keep us from the abyss, I think.
With the cheque I'll buy a trellis, or a tree.
There are so many of you here to thank.

And unaccustomed as I am to drink,
I toast you all who follow me
– There are so many of you here to thank –
In dreaming down to Morden, via Bank.

Up-Hill

Does the road wind up-hill all the way?
  Yes, to the very end.
Will the day's journey take the whole long day?
  From morn to night, my friend.

But is there for the night a resting-place?
  A roof for when the slow dark hours begin.
May not the darkness hide it from my face?
  You cannot miss that inn.

Shall I meet other wayfarers at night?
  Those who have gone before.
Then must I knock, or call when just in sight?
  They will not keep you standing at that door.

Shall I find comfort, travel-sore and weak?
  Of labour you shall find the sum.
Will there be beds for me and all who seek?
  Yea, beds for all who come.

Warning

When I am an old woman I shall wear purple
With a red hat which doesn't go, and doesn't suit me,
And I shall spend my pension on brandy and summer gloves
And satin sandals, and say we've no money for butter.
I shall sit down on the pavement when I'm tired
And gobble up samples in shops and press alarm bells
And run my stick along the public railings
And make up for the sobriety of my youth.
I shall go out in my slippers in the rain
And pick the flowers in other people's gardens
And learn to spit.

You can wear terrible shirts and grow more fat
And eat three pounds of sausages at a go
Or only bread and pickle for a week
And hoard pens and pencils and beermats and things in boxes.

But now we must have clothes that keep us dry
And pay our rent and not swear in the street
And set a good example for the children.
We will have friends to dinner and read the papers.

But maybe I ought to practise a little now?
So people who know me are not too shocked and surprised
When suddenly I am old and start to wear purple.

Much Madness is divinest Sense –
To a discerning Eye –
Much Sense – the starkest Madness –
'Tis the Majority
In this, as All, prevail –
Assent – And you are sane –
Demur – you're straightway dangerous –
And handled with a Chain –

FRANCES CORNFORD (1886–1960)

Childhood

I used to think that grown-up people chose
To have stiff backs and wrinkles round their nose,
And veins like small fat snakes on either hand,
On purpose to be grand.
Till through the banisters I watched one day
My great-aunt Etty's friend who was going away,
And how her onyx beads had come unstrung.
I saw her grope to find them as they rolled;
And then I knew that she was helplessly old,
As I was helplessly young.

Delta

If you have taken this rubble for my past
raking through it for fragments you could sell
know that I long ago moved on
deeper into the heart of the matter.

If you think you can grasp me, think again:
my story flows in more than one direction
a delta springing from the riverbed
with its five fingers spread.

Song

Fall, leaves, fall; die, flowers, away;
Lengthen night and shorten day;
Every leaf speaks bliss to me
Fluttering from the autumn tree.
I shall smile when wreaths of snow
Blossom where the rose should grow;
I shall sing when night's decay
Ushers in a drearier day.

Matinee

Grandma, whisper, everybody's turning around.
– Well is she being thrown out of the convent?
No, she's just going to be a governess for a while.
– What does she have on?
A brown dress, hat and she's carrying a suitcase.
– Where's she going, is she walking or what?
Yeah, she's walking to the house where she's got the job.
– Why didn't they pick her up in a carriage?
So she could sing a song on the way.
– Is this a true story?
I guess so.
– Well I bet they picked her up.
Now she's meeting the family.
– She marries the father, Ingrid told me.
He's very handsome and rich.
– I thought you said she was still a nun.

ELIZABETH JENNINGS (b. 1926)

One Flesh

Lying apart now, each in a separate bed,
He with a book, keeping the light on late,
She like a girl dreaming of childhood,
All men elsewhere – it is as if they wait
Some new event: the book he holds unread,
Her eyes fixed on the shadows overhead.

Tossed up like flotsam from a former passion,
How cool they lie. They hardly ever touch,
Or if they do it is like a confession
Of having little feeling – or too much.
Chastity faces them, a destination
For which their whole lives were a preparation.

Strangely apart, yet strangely close together,
Silence between them like a thread to hold
And not wind in. And time itself's a feather
Touching them gently. Do they know they're old,
These two who are my father and my mother
Whose fire from which I came, has now grown cold?

A House of Mercy

It was a house of female habitation,
Two ladies fair inhabited the house,
And they were brave. For although Fear knocked loud
Upon the door, and said he must come in,
They did not let him in.

There were also two feeble babes, two girls,
That Mrs S. had by her husband had,
He soon left them and went away to sea,
Nor sent them money, nor came home again
Except to borrow back
Her Naval Officer's Wife's Allowance from Mrs S.
Who gave it him at once, she thought she should.

There was also the ladies' aunt
And babes' great aunt, a Mrs Martha Hearn Clode,
And she was elderly.
These ladies put their money all together
And so we lived.

I was the younger of the feeble babes
And when I was a child my mother died
And later Great Aunt Martha Hearn Clode died
And later still my sister went away.

Now I am old I tend my mother's sister
The noble aunt who so long tended us,
Faithful and True her name is. Tranquil.
Also Sardonic. And I tend the house.

It is a house of female habitation
A house expecting strength as it is strong
A house of aristocratic mould that looks apart
When tears fall; counts despair
Derisory. Yet it has kept us well. For all its faults,
If they are faults, of sternness and reserve,
It is a Being of warmth I think; at heart
A house of mercy.

EMILY BRONTË (1818–48)

The Old Stoic

Riches I hold in light esteem
And Love I laugh to scorn
And Lust of Fame was but a dream
That vanished with the morn –

And if I pray – the only prayer
That moves my lips for me
Is – 'Leave the heart that now I bear
And give me liberty.'

Yes, as my swift days near their goal
'Tis all that I implore –
In life and death, a chainless soul
With courage to endure!

Exchanging Gifts

Your fingers,
skilled with wood,
could fashion furniture;
made me a doll's house once
when toys were scarce,
small casualties of war.
I heard you hammering
each night,
did not appreciate your gifts
of time and craftsmanship.

Your hands,
now twisted, gnarled with age,
will tremble as they pass a cup,
yet you produce
smooth polished bowls,
rounded and begging
to be touched.
Your turning lathe
gives life to ancient apple trees,
you make old, knotted oak
conform to your design.

My way with words
you never valued,
never understood –
until today
I find you trying to write
a tribute to a friend,
now dead.
Taking your speech,
coarse-grained as rough-hewn pine,
I carve and shape,
then plane and polish language,

order your thoughts,
give tongue to love
and fill your empty hands
as you filled mine.

ANNE STEVENSON (b. 1933)

Talking Sense to my Senses

Old ears and eyes, so long my patient friends,
For you this silicon nerve and resin lens.
Guides when I heard and saw, yet deaf and blind
Stumbled astray in the mazes of my mind,
Let me assist you now I've lived to see
Far in the dark of what I have to be.

Shunted outside the hubbub of exchange,
Knowledge arrives, articulate and strange,
Voice without breath, light without sun or switch
Beamed from the pulse of an old awareness which
Tells me to age by love and not to cling
To ears, eyes, teeth, knees, hands – or any thing.

Sonnet

What lips my lips have kissed, and where, and why,
I have forgotten, and what arms have lain
Under my head till morning; but the rain
Is full of ghosts tonight, that tap and sigh
Upon the glass and listen for reply,
And in my heart there stirs a quiet pain
For unremembered lads that not again
Will turn to me at midnight with a cry.
Thus in the winter stands the lonely tree,
Nor knows what birds have vanished one by one,
Yet knows its boughs more silent than before:
I cannot say what loves have come and gone,
I only know that summer sang in me
A little while, that in me sings no more.

TOVE DITLEVSEN (1917–76)
TRANSLATED BY NADIA CHRISTENSEN

The Old Folk

The old folk do not lay
plans far into the future
do not postpone anything until
the day after tomorrow.

In the evening they burn
letters in the fireplace.
Each newborn morning
they thank God for life
which is no longer
a matter of course.

If they mention Death
everyone cheerfully protests
which makes them
more alone.
With no one can they talk about
this great
at-birth-ordained
event.

In the bleak mid-winter

CHRISTINA ROSSETTI (1830–94)

Song

When I am dead, my dearest,
  Sing no sad songs for me;
Plant thou no roses at my head,
  Nor shady cypress tree:
Be the green grass above me
  With showers and dewdrops wet:
And if thou wilt, remember,
  And if thou wilt, forget.

I shall not see the shadows,
  I shall not fear the rain;
I shall not hear the nightingale
  Sing on as if in pain:
And dreaming through the twilight
  That doth not rise nor set,
Haply I may remember,
  And haply may forget.

Mrs Malone

Mrs Malone
Lived hard by a wood
All on her lonesome
As nobody should.
With her crust on a plate
And her pot on the coal
And none but herself
To converse with, poor soul.
In a shawl and a hood
She got sticks out-o'door,
On a bit of old sacking
She slept on the floor,
And nobody nobody
Asked how she fared
Or knew how she managed,
For nobody cared.
    Why make a pother
    About an old crone?
    What for should they bother
    With Mrs Malone?

One Monday in winter
With snow on the ground
So thick that a footstep
Fell without sound,
She heard a faint frostbitten
Peck on the pane
And went to the window
To listen again.

There sat a cock-sparrow
Bedraggled and weak,
With half-open eyelid
And ice on his beak.

She threw up the sash
And she took the bird in,
And mumbled and fumbled it
Under her chin
  'Ye're all of a smother,
  Ye're fair overblown!
  I've room fer another,'
  Said Mrs Malone.

Come Tuesday while eating
Her dry morning slice
With the sparrow a-picking
('Ain't company nice!')
She heard on her doorpost
A curious scratch,
And there was a cat
With its claw on the latch.
It was hungry and thirsty
And thin as a lath,
It mewed and it mowed
On the slithery path.
She threw the door open
And warmed up some pap,
And huddled and cuddled it
In her old lap.
  'There, there, little brother,
  Ye poor skin-an'-bone,
  There's room fer another,'
  Said Mrs Malone.

Come Wednesday while all of them
Crouched on the mat
With a crumb for the sparrow,
A sip for the cat,
There was a wailing and whining
Outside in the wood,
And there sat a vixen
With six of her brood.
She was haggard and ragged

And worn to a shred,
And her half-dozen babies
Were only half-fed,
But Mrs Malone, crying
'My! ain't they sweet!'
Happed them and lapped them
And gave them to eat.
    'You warm yerself, mother,
    Ye're cold as a stone!
    There's room fer another,'
    Said Mrs Malone.

Come Thursday a donkey
Stepped in off the road
With sores on his withers
From bearing a load.
Come Friday when icicles
Pierced the white air
Down from the mountainside
Lumbered a bear.
For each she had something,
If little, to give –
'Lord knows, the poor critters
Must all of 'em live,'
She gave them her sacking,
Her hood and her shawl,
Her loaf and her teapot –
She gave them her all.
    'What with one thing and t'other
    Me fambily's grown,
    And there's room fer another,'
    Said Mrs Malone.

Come Saturday evening
When time was to sup
Mrs Malone
Had forgot to sit up.
The cat said meeow,
And the sparrow said peep,

The vixen, she's sleeping,
The bear, let her sleep.
On the back of the donkey
They bore her away,
Through trees and up mountains
Beyond night and day,
Till come Sunday morning
They brought her in state
Through the last cloudbank
As far as the Gate.
    'Who is it,' asked Peter,
    'You have with you there?'
    And donkey and sparrow,
    Cat, vixen, and bear

Exclaimed, 'Do you tell us
Up here she's unknown?
It's our mother, God bless us!
It's Mrs Malone,
Whose havings were few
And whose holding was small
And whose heart was so big
It had room for us all.'
Then Mrs Malone
Of a sudden awoke,
She rubbed her two eyeballs
And anxiously spoke:
'Where am I, to goodness,
And what do I see?
My dear, let's turn back,
This ain't no place fer me!'
But Peter said, 'Mother
Go in to the Throne.
There's room for another
One, Mrs Malone.'

Cold in the Earth

Cold in the earth – and the deep snow piled above thee,
Far, far removed, cold in the dreary grave!
Have I forgot, my only Love, to love thee,
Severed at last by Time's all-severing wave?

Now, when alone, do my thoughts no longer hover
Over the mountains, on that northern shore,
Resting their wings where heath and fern-leaves cover
Thy noble heart for ever, ever more?

Cold in the earth – and fifteen wild Decembers,
From those brown hills, have melted into spring:
Faithful, indeed, is the spirit that remembers
After such years of change and suffering!

Sweet Love of youth, forgive, if I forget thee,
While the world's tide is bearing me along;
Other desires and other hopes beset me,
Hopes which obscure, but cannot do thee wrong!

No later light has lightened up my heaven,
No second morn has ever shone for me;
All my life's bliss from thy dear life was given,
All my life's bliss is in the grave with thee.

But, when the days of golden dreams had perished,
And even Despair was powerless to destroy;
Then did I learn how existence could be cherished,
Strengthened, and fed without the aid of joy.

Then did I check the tears of useless passion –
Weaned my young soul from yearning after thine;
Sternly denied its burning wish to hasten
Down to that tomb already more than mine.

And, even yet, I dare not let it languish,
Dare not indulge in memory's rapturous pain;
Once drinking deep of that divinest anguish,
How could I seek the empty world again?

KATHARINE MIDDLETON

....

Her Death

Her death, and the soot-blackened hospital wall
ten minutes behind him,
he comes down the deserted road
to the bus-stop where no one's waiting.

The concrete shelter is roofed and open-fronted;
shaped, he's thought often these last few weeks,
like a pavilion for spectators
at a tournament, at games.

Now it flies great flags – night's navy-blue,
white pennons of the bleak street-lights,
and the colourless, all-coloured
flags of chaos.

At the edge of the world
he stands looking out on the mists of space.
Out there the arena, the tiers of seats,
lie empty.

The bus from Andromeda arrives.
The return-half of his ticket will take him
somewhere, even though the place he set out from
will no longer be there.

The Death of Adam

I saw it coming,
The cold.
It must have been coming on a long time.
Ever since I'd known him.

Not surprising, really,
With him come up from the dust
And me from the bone.
Still, it was odd,
Watching it actually happen.
Everything sags; did you know?
I didn't know.

Teeth fall out, and then the face falls in.
Skin
Withers and wrinkles and shrivels like an apple
(Yes, like an apple)
And the top of the skull
(Where the hair and the brains keep complicated house together)
Becomes
Plain, smooth, simple,
Unoccupied by anything.

And he couldn't walk at all, nor talk at all
(We had to stop arguing about whose fault it was)
And the sun made his eyes hurt
And he had to leave the world that belonged to him
And the animals he'd given a name to
And the wife that was part of him,
To become a kind of collapse,
A remnant, something remembered,
Not all there any more.

He was always first at everything
And now
The first man ever to be dead.
Perhaps, as gardeners,
We should have learned from the leaves
What it means to be deciduous.

Will it always be just like this
For the rest of us?
Or must I look forward
To a separate, feminine, suitable
Method of disappearance?
Middle-aged, but still naked
To man-stare and God-stare
Covering myself up with my hands and my long grey hair,
Breasts falling like apples
And the small pool of darkness
Inside me
Gone dry?

Farewell

Farewell to Thee! But not farewell
To all my fondest thoughts of Thee;
Within my heart they still shall dwell
And they shall cheer and comfort me.

Life seems more sweet that Thou didst live
And men more true that Thou wert one;
Nothing is lost that Thou didst give,
Nothing destroyed that Thou hast done.

PATRICIA BEER (b. 1924)

Called Home

'Called Home' the Plymouth Brethren used to say
When someone died. Warm, bright corridors
Led to eternal domesticity
And from outside we heard the sound of tears
Being wiped away by God. Shall we gather
At the river? In the sweet by-and-by?
Yes, I sang then. Beyond the bright blue sky
Dead families would always be together.

Loving an atheist is my hope currently.
Believers cannot help. I must have some
Ally who will keep non-company
With me in a non-life, a fellow tombstone
Stuck senseless in cold grass, squinnying down
At father, uncle, grandfather, called home.

Dirge Without Music

I am resigned to the shutting away of loving hearts in the
    hard ground
So it is, and so it will be, for so it has been, time out of mind:
Into the darkness they go, the wise and the lovely. Crowned
With lilies and with laurel they go: but I am not resigned.

Lovers and thinkers, into the earth with you.
Be one with the dull, the indiscriminate dust.
A fragment of what you felt, of what you knew,
A formula, a phrase remains – but the best is lost.

The answers quick and keen, the honest look, the laughter,
    the love –
They are gone. They have gone to feed the roses. Elegant and
    curled
Is the blossom. Fragrant is the blossom. I know. But I do
    not approve.
More precious was the light in your eyes than all the roses in
    the world.

Down, down, down into the darkness of the grave
Gently they go, the beautiful, the tender, the kind:
Quietly they go, the intelligent, the witty, the brave.
I know. But I do not approve. And I am not resigned.

A Christmas Carol

In the bleak mid-winter
    Frosty wind made moan,
Earth stood hard as iron,
    Water like a stone;
Snow had fallen, snow on snow,
    Snow on snow,
In the bleak mid-winter
    Long ago.

Our God, Heaven cannot hold Him
    Nor earth sustain;
Heaven and earth shall flee away
    When he comes to reign:
In the bleak mid-winter
    A stable-place sufficed
The Lord God Almighty
    Jesus Christ.

Enough for Him, whom cherubim
    Worship night and day,
A breastful of milk
    And a mangerful of hay;
Enough for Him, whom angels
    Fall down before,
The ox and ass and camel
    Which adore.

Angels and archangels
    May have gathered there,
Cherubim and seraphim
    Thronged the air;
But only His mother
    In her maiden bliss
Worshipped the Beloved
    With a kiss.

What can I give Him.
    Poor as I am?
If I were a shepherd
    I would bring a lamb,
If I were a Wise Man
    I would do my part, –
Yet what I can I give Him,
    Give my heart.

JANET CAIRD (b. 1913)

Let the Snow Cover Her

Let the snow cover her.
She is too old to follow the sledge
and her fingers too stiff
to hold the bone-needle and stitch
the silk-soft sealskin.
It is years and years since she bore her children
in the warm snow-house on the ice-floe.
Here in the hollow
the down of the snow-drift
the silence and cold
will lull her to sleep.
Let the snow cover her.

Last Rites

This is the day
we have postponed,
fearing disfavour
from beyond the grave,
your spirit watching
from a corner of the room.

So many clothes
in musty cupboards,
drawers closed tight,
dresses I don't remember,
coats which you forgot;
shoes spilling out from boxes
stacked on dusty shelves.

I make a pile
of crumbling peppermints
and crumpled tissues
plucked from pockets
shaped by knotted hands.

He keeps a handbag
filled with secrets
and the last sad trivia
of your life,
then bids me take your rings;
a diamond promise,
golden vow
and circle of eternity.
The rest I leave –
fake gems which glitter,
winking in the sudden light.
I close the lacquered lid,
returning them to night.

We work as quickly as we can.
He flinches at the pain
of opened wounds,
I hide my guilt
at smooth unbroken skin
until my fumbling fingers
find your mirror
and I bleed,
cut deeply by
a small reflection
of myself.

VALENTINE ACKLAND (1906–68)

Life Strikes

Life strikes like a clock, and the hour on the beat of the strike
Is here and is mine and is gone before the echo is done.
In that moment alone I held life within me, to make
One line, one rhyme, one living word, and begone –
But instead, entranced, I gazed till the hammer should fall on the bell,
And it fell –

ACKNOWLEDGEMENTS

The publishers would like to thank the following for their permission to reproduce copyright material.

Gillian Allnutt for 'Convent', first published in *Beginning the Avocado* (Virago 1987); Virago Press for 'Televised' by Maya Angelou from *Complete Collected Poems of Maya Angelou*; Curtis Brown Ltd, London for 'February' on behalf of Margaret Atwood © O.W. Toad Ltd 1995; Elizabeth Bartlett for 'Stretch Marks' and 'Themes for Women' from *Two Women Dancing, New and Selected Poems* (Bloodaxe 1995) re-printed by permission of Bloodaxe and Elizabeth Bartlett; Paul A. North, literary executor of the Estate of Vera Bax for 'To Billy, My Son' by Vera Bax; Carcanet Press Ltd for 'Called Home', 'The Faithful Wife' and 'Mating Calls' by Patricia Beer from *Collected Poems*; Commonword Ltd for 'Division' and 'Song of the Woman Past Forty' first published in *Crocus Five Women Poets* (Crocus); Connie Bensley for 'Politeness' from *Choosing To Be a Swan* (Bloodaxe Books Ltd); The Estate of Mary Desiree Anderson for 'The Black-Out'; Mabel Esther Allan for 'Immensity' and 'I Saw a Broken Town' from *Chaos of the Night* (Virago 1984); Reed Books for 'War Casualty in April' by Frances Bellerby from *Plash Mill and Other Poems* by Frances Bellerby (William Heinemann); Carcanet Press Ltd for 'Night Feed' by Eavan Boland from *Night Feed*; Paul Berry, her literary executor, for 'The Lament of the Demobilised', 'The War Generation: Ave' and 'The War Generation: Vale' by Vera Brittain; The Lomond Press (Kinnesswood) for 'Leave poem' by Anne Bulley; Faber & Faber Ltd for 'Giving Up Smoking', 'Message' and 'Rondeau Redoublé' from *Making Cocoa for Kingsley Amis* and 'The Uncertainty of the Poet' from *Serious Concerns* by Wendy Cope; Random House UK Ltd and the Estate of Frances Cornford for 'Autumn Blitz' and 'Childhood' by Frances Cornford from *Collected Poems* (Jonathan Cape); Peters, Fraser & Dunlop Group Ltd for 'The Other Side of the Story' by Catherine

Lucy Czerkwska; Gyldendalske Boghandel for 'The Old Folk' by Tove Ditlevsen; Bloodaxe Books Ltd for 'A Plain Girl' by Freda Downie; A P Watt Ltd for 'Safe Period' by Helen Dunmore; Seren Books for 'Jugged Hare' and 'Menopause' by Jean Earle from *Selected Poems* (Seren 1990); Ruth Fainlight for 'Handbag'; Peterloo Poets for 'Not My Best Side' © U. A. Fanthorpe from *Side Effects* (Peterloo Poets 1978), 'Fanfare' © U. A. Fanthorpe from *Standing To* (Peterloo Poets 1982) and 'The Poet's Companion' © U. A. Fanthorpe from *Neck-Verse* (Peterloo Poets 1992); David Higham Associates for 'Mrs Malone' by Eleanor Farjeon from *Silver Sand and Snow* (Michael Joseph); Random House UK Ltd for 'Crab Apple Jelly' by Vicki Feaver from *The Handless Maiden* (Jonathan Cape); Carcanet Press Ltd for 'Getting Older' and 'Urban Lyric' by Elaine Fenstein from *Selected Poems*; Commonword Ltd for 'The Apex' by Marguerite Gazeley first published in *Crocus Five Women Poets* (Crocus); Pamela Gillilan for 'Doorsteps' and 'Home is the Hunter' from *All-Steel Traveller, new and selected poems by Pamela Gillilan* (Bloodaxe Books Ltd, 1994); Louise Gluck for 'Flowering Plum'; The Executors of the Estate of Virginia Graham for 'It's All Very Well Now' by Virginia Graham; Polygon for 'For Eileen' from *Original Prints Vol 11* (Polygon 1987); Sheil Land Associates for 'The Gate of the Year' by M. Louise Haskins; Phoebe Hesketh for 'Post-War Christmas' from *Lean Forward Spring!* (Sidgwick and Jackson 1948); Selima Hill for 'The Unsuccessful Wedding Night'; © Alan Holden for 'Seaman, 1941' and 'Stopping Places' by Molly Holden; David Higham Associates for 'Friendship', 'Song at the Beginning of Autumn' and 'One Flesh' by Elizabeth Jennings from *Collected Poems* (Carcanet); Bloodaxe Books Ltd for 'Warning' by Jenny Joseph; Sylvia Kantaris for 'Annunciation' from *The Tenth Muse*, 1983, re-issued by Menhir 1986; Jackie Kay for 'From Other Lovers: When You Move Out' from *From Other Lovers* (Bloodaxe 1993); Fran Landesman for 'Personals' and 'Shoes'; Laurence Pollinger Ltd, New Directions Publishing Corporation for 'Idyll' by Denise Levertov from *Evening Train* (Bloodaxe Books Ltd); A. P. Watt Ltd for 'After a Warrant Sale', 'Box Room', 'The Empty Song', 'Fin', 'The Hickie', 'How Have I Been?', 'A Letter', 'The Other Woman' and 'Poem for My Sister' by Liz Lochhead, all from *Dreaming Frankenstein*; Sarah Maguire for 'May Day, 1986'; Vasa D. Milhailovich for 'For Lies Spoken Out of Kindness' by Desanka Maksimović; Mermaid Books for 'Her Death' by Katherine Middleton; A. M. Heath and the Estate of Edna St Vincent Millay for 'Sonnet' and 'Dirge Without Music' by Edna St Vincent Millay; Charlotte Mitchell for 'The Passing of the Telegram'; Elma Mitchell for

INDEX OF FIRST LINES

INDEX OF POETS